WEEPING may last for the night
But there is a song of JOY
in the morning
Psalm 30: 5

Sing me a Song to SOAR
Finding hope in our redemptive stories

Dr Julie Morsillo
Community Psychologist

SING ME A SONG TO SOAR
Finding Hope in Our Redemptive Stories

Copyright © 2024 Julie Morsillo. All rights reserved. Except for brief quotations in critical publications or reviews, no part of this book may be reproduced in any manner without prior written permission from the publisher. Write: Permissions, Wipf and Stock Publishers, 199 W. 8th Ave., Suite 3, Eugene, OR 97401.

Resource Publications
An Imprint of Wipf and Stock Publishers
199 W. 8th Ave., Suite 3
Eugene, OR 97401

www.wipfandstock.com

PAPERBACK ISBN: 979-8-3852-3243-7
HARDCOVER ISBN: 979-8-3852-3244-4
EBOOK ISBN: 979-8-3852-3245-1

Sing me a song to soar: Finding hope in our redemptive stories

*By **Dr Julie Morsillo** PhD, Community Psychologist, 2024.*

Preface

Life can be very challenging at times, with dark nights of the soul. We often need support to make our way through the tough times and find the light of the morning.

This **handbook for counsellors** offers some helpful tools to support others through their dark times, to find hope in their redemptive stories for some healing. A hope that helps us find a story song to SOAR in life.

Introduction: **Stories have power**

Part 1: **Stories of personal meaning** in life with

Part 2: **Other respectful relationships** beside us

Part 3: **A supportive community** encircling us and

Part 4: **Restorative** time in **nature**

This handbook provides some insights into uplifting hopeful narrative theories on finding personal meaning and ways to connect with others and with nature. It also includes links to videos and further readings to learn more. Plus, some poetry and many practical worksheets with prompts, to help reflect on various aspects of life, as we seek to find more hopeful redemptive stories to soar in life.

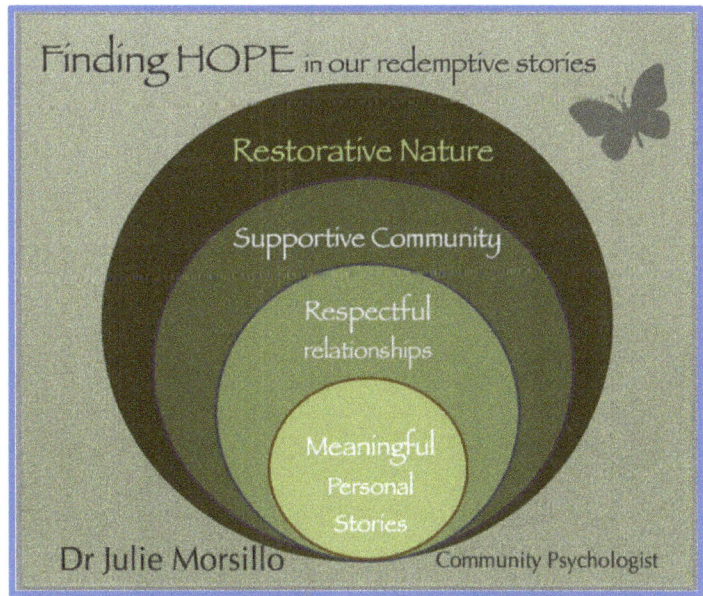

Figure 1: Finding redemptive stories by Dr Julie Morsillo

CONTENTS

- PREFACE 3
- **INTRODUCTION – STORIES HAVE POWER** 6
  - Inspirations 6
  - Finding redemptive stories 7
  - Stories have power 8
- **PART 1 – STORIES OF PERSONAL MEANING IN LIFE** 13
  - 1.1 Care of own soul and body 14
  - 1.2 Positive Psychology and wellbeing 20
  - 1.3 Personal meaning in life 27
  - 1.4 Gratitude journal 30
  - 1.5 Finding meaning after loss 33
  - 1.6 Gratitude for hopeful life stories 35
  - 1.7 Narrative therapy for hopeful life stories 41
  - 1.8 Self-compassion and Compassion focused therapy 52
  - 1.9 Finding personal meaning with children 59
  - 1.10 Finding personal meaning work with youth 60
- **PART 2 – OTHER RESPECTFUL RELATIONSHIPS BESIDE US** 61
  - 2.1 Life in relationship with others 62
  - 2.2 Appreciating life and work 63
  - 2.3 Communicating positively well 65
  - 2.4 The Shark Cage – disrespectful relationships 67
  - 2.5 Power Threat Meaning Framework 70
  - 2.6 Dealing with difficult relationships 72
  - 2.7 Respectful relationships stories 74
  - 2.8 Biography and Dignity Therapy 75
- **PART 3 – A SUPPORTIVE COMMUNITY ENCIRCLING US** 77
  - 3.1 Caring community services 79
  - 3.2 Meaningful community groups 82
- **PART 4 – RESTORATIVE TIME IN NATURE** 86
  - 4.1 Appreciating connections to nature 87
  - 4.2 Creating in nature 88
  - 4.3 Restoring nature 88
  - 4.4 Living in nature 88
  - 4.5 Eco-therapy or nature therapy 90
  - 4.6 Narrative walks 92
  - 4.7 Restoring nature ideas 94
- **REFERENCES** 96
  - Useful Websites 98
  - Video Links 99
  - Poems & Permissions 101

TABLE of WORKSHEETS

Worksheet A – Special story in life 12
Worksheet B – Calm the Soul 16
Worksheet C – Relaxed Movement 19
Worksheet D – Inspiring Music 22
Worksheet E – Empowerment story 26
Worksheet F – Finding meaning in Life 28
Worksheet G – Gratitude Journal 31
Worksheet H – Meaning After Loss 34
Worksheet I – Tree of Life metaphor 43
Worksheet J – Team of Life metaphor 45
Worksheet K – Kite of Life metaphor 47
Worksheet L – Crossing the River metaphor 49
Worksheet M – Life Certificate metaphor 51
Worksheet N – Self–Compassion 53
Worksheet O – Compassion Focused Therapy 55
Worksheet P – Appreciative Inquiry 64
Worksheet Q – Communicating Well 66
Worksheet R – Coercive Control 69
Worksheet S – Power Threat Meaning Framework 71
Worksheet T – Dignity Therapy 76
Worksheet U – Community Supports 81
Worksheet V – Community Garden 84
Worksheet W – Community Groups 85
Worksheet X – Restorative Time in Nature 89
Worksheet Y – Nature Therapy 91
Worksheet Z – Narrative Walk 93

Disclaimer:

These worksheets, and other advice in this handbook, are offered as suggestions only, to perhaps use with people who are distressed about the challenges in life that we all face at times.

However, if a person is extremely distressed with ongoing mental health issues, that adversely affect their functioning in everyday life, they may need further support from medical health professionals, for appropriate medication to stabilise their condition.

Introduction – Stories have power
Inspirations

Dedication to Rosalie Joy
To my late younger sister, Rosalie Joy (1958-2023), who taught me how to find my own voice, my own song to soar. Despite her constant physical and emotional pain, beginning in childhood with severe asthma, and later also migraines, that with other complications led to a continuous migraine in the last seven years of her life.

Yet, my sister, taught me how to stand up for myself and to problem solve. She could make me laugh, when I was sad, with the hilarious ways she told stories about life. Rosalie Joy also taught me the enjoyment of creative spaces in life: celebrating special times; a garden to sooth the soul; beautiful spaces in the home; colourful hippy clothes; arts and crafts to enhance life; boating on smooth or choppy seas; road trips to visit aunts and uncles, and places of natural beauty; and singing in harmony together, like when we sang acapella at our Dad's funeral, the traditional song, *I'll fly away*.

Inspirations from other life experiences
An early memory of singing a solo as a small child in Sutherland Baptist Church, Sydney - *This little light of mine, I'm going let it shine.* Then a few years later, after several changes of schools interstate, in the early 60s, I began to stutter badly, but thankfully a kind neighbour in Brisbane, gave me free speech therapy.

A gap year, after high school, in early 70s, following my missionary parents to the highlands of Papua New Guinea, talking my way into teaching at a primary school, giving literacy and piano tuition.

Newly married had a three year 'honeymoon' in Victor Harbour, going to Bible College of South Australia in mid-70s, a popular place for honeymooners. First child was born there too, with walks along the rocky beach shore every day.

As a young adult in the 80s, caring for foster children and cottage children with husband and own two children in Melbourne, whist doing part-time psychology studies at Victoria University.

Equal opportunity and human rights work with the state government in the 90s, with post-grad study in adolescent & child psychology (Uni of Melb), and later a Masters of Social Science, in International Development (RMIT).

Working with refugee youth for PhD research in 2000s using appreciative inquiry to celebrate their own cultural heritage and connect with local communities. Plus working with refugees as counselling co-ordinator at the *Asylum Seeker Resource Centre*, Melbourne.

Learning narrative therapy at the Dulwich Centre, Adelaide. Teaching narrative therapy to counsellors in Melbourne, plus guest workshops in Cambodia with counsellors, and with counsellors of holocaust survivors and their children, in The Great Synagogue of Prague, Czech.

Traumatic fall on black ice in Czech mountains with a broken wrist (2019) and fainting on a fire trail in the Blue Mountains, NSW (2022).

Tragedies of a world-wide pandemic in the most locked down place, with more time to appreciate nature, indoor and outdoor plants and a make-shift garden studio. Long Covid with little energy, and recently the death of my dear sister, my confidante.

Julie & sister Rosalie Joy in 2015 before her illness

Memorial rose garden for sister 2023

Finding redemptive stories

by Laura Boys, counselling student, 2021

Holding hope and finding a song to sing, through the dark times of our lives, the storms of our lives, when we feel lost or broken, can be tough. But with support we can our redemptive stories to shine a light on a way forward.

Sing me a song to soar

This handbook on finding our own song to soar in life, with our own *redemptive stories*, offers some practical ways to find hope for yourself and perhaps support others to find hope in their lives. This book can be used as a handbook for personal work or for ways to support counsellors helping others.

Personal meaningful stories

Firstly, to consider ways to strengthen personal stories that are meaningful, which are often lost in our thoughts, as we tend to dwell on the problems and pressures in our lives, to order to solve those issues. Of course, we do need to spend time resolving issues of concern.

However, it can be most helpful, to spend time recalling the hopeful moments of our lives, the times when we felt treasured and supported, and could enjoy life, at least a little.

This handbook provides an opportunity to reflect on our hopeful stories, the times when life offered opportunities, and we felt the beauty of nature and the support of those around us. Perhaps only for fleeting moments, perhaps long ago. But reflecting on these times can give us renewed hope in life, and maybe even reconnect with positive affirming interests and supports in our lives.

Note: Laura Boys, author of this introductory section, studied counselling at Eastern College Australia and assisted me in the early days of writing this handbook in late 2021 to early 2022.

Respectful relationship stories

Secondly, to consider ways to strengthen respectful relationship stories. Often our life issues are problematic because we don't have respectful relationships with those around us. We may be good at being respectful, but not so good as demanding respect from others. We all deserve to be treated with respect and dignity. No-one deserves to be belittled, or coerced, or isolated from other friends and family. This can lead to guilt and shame, and then infects our relationships in unhelpful ways.

So this handbook may provide some ideas on ways to be more respectful and caring of those around us, and often more importantly, to insist that others treat us with the respect and dignity that everyone deserves. Learning to see red flags, learning to say no to disrespect or coercion, learning to give up guilt and shame, for more hopeful and caring relationships with others around us.

Supportive community stories

Thirdly, this handbook seeks to show the importance of supportive communities that help us to have hope and thrive. Good housing, good health services, and educational pathways to support us to reach our potential and be a valued member of the community.

We need to feel valued, in order to add value, to our local communities and the wider community. Educational pathways and community programs promoting skills for employment and health lifestyles for healthy bodies and healthy relationships.

Restorative times in nature stories

Finally, but more importantly in the long term, we need to consider ways to restore and renew nature, so that we have a place to live and breath and offer our ourselves, our children and our grandchildren a healthy future.

Stories have power

by Laura Boys, counselling student, 2021

Stories have power. Reading fictional stories enables us to find ourselves with the characters and not feel so alone. Stories provide a mirror to look at oneself and reflect on what kind of people we want to be. They provide a safe space to explore complex emotions through metaphors and fictional scenarios and characters.

We also each have our own personal story. A story that is shaped by the people we encounter day-to-day, societal norms that permeate our perspectives and tell us how we should behave to be accepted, and our own values that guide our decision making, beliefs and intentions.

The most important questions to ask yourself are:

Is my story empowering or inhibiting?

Is what I see the whole story?

We are story

Quote by Richard Wagamese, Ojibwe, 2011

"All that we are is Story. From the moment we are born to the time we continue on our spirit journey we are involved in the creation of the story of our time here. It is what we arrive with. It is all we leave behind. We are not the things we accumulate. We are not the things we deem important. We are story. All of us.

What comes to matter then is the creation of the best possible story we can, while we're here; you, me, us, together. When we can do that, and we take the time to share those stories with each other, we get bigger inside, we see each other, we recognize our kinship — we change the world one story at a time."

Richard Wagamese
Richard Wagamese (1955-2017) was an Ojibwe (first nations) Canadian author and journalist.

Richard Wagamese speech
Richard Wagamese 2015 Matt Cohen Award speech - https://youtube/t0z9rYHbQ8E?si=G-Ir14CZM_Y1NCbZ

Richard Wagamese book
Wagamese, R. (2011). *One story, one song*. Douglas & McIntyre.

Story of hope not fear
Quote by Nelson Mandela, 1994

"May your choices reflect your hopes, not your fears …There can be no greater gift than that of giving one's time and energy helping others without expecting anything in return … For to be free is not merely to cast off one's chains but to live in a way that respects and enhances the freedom of others."

> THERE IS NO
> FEAR
> IN LOVE
> PERFECT LOVE
> CASTS OUT FEAR
> 1 John 4: 18

Nelson Mandela
He was an anti-apartheid activist, lawyer, and political prisoner for 27 years, yet forgave whose who imprisoned him, and later became the first black President of South Africa.

Nelson Mandela book
Mandela, N. (2009). *Long walk to freedom.* Flash Point/Roaring Brook Press.

President Nelson Mandela's Inaugural speech (1994)
www.youtube.com/watch?v=pJiXu4q__VU

Life stories of redemption
Quote by Prof Dan P. McAdams, 2006

"We are all tellers of tales and we seek to provide our scattered and often confusing experiences with a sense of coherence by arranging the episodes of our lives . . . Narrative identity is a person's internalized and evolving life story, integrating the reconstructed past and imagined future to provide life with some degree of unity and purpose…. Research into the relation between life stories and adaptation shows that narrators who **find redemptive meanings in suffering and adversity and who construct life stories that feature themes of personal agency and exploration,** tend to enjoy higher levels of mental health, well-being, and maturity."

Dr Dan McAdams book
McAdams, D. P. (2006). *The redemptive self: Stories Americans live by.* Oxford University Press.

Lecture by Dr Dan McAdams
Narrative approaches to the self (2022)
www.youtube.com/watch?v=C1eEpK23Hvg

> It is here that we encounter the central theme of existentialism: to live is to suffer, to survive is to find meaning in the suffering
> Viktor Frankl.

Prof Viktor Frankl book
Frankl, V. E. (1950). *Man's search for meaning: An introduction to logotherapy.* Beacon Press.

Prof Viktor Frankl interview
Why meaning matters (1963)
www.youtube.com/watch?v=BB8X-Go7lgw

Finding redemptive story after loss
       Poem by Dr Julie Morsillo, 2022

Living in a world of wonder
But disruptions come to rock our world
Pandemics, bushfires, floods
Broken body with illness or accident
Abused body with too many threats

Disruptions can take us to dark places
Down the valley of the shadow of death
Near death experiences
Death of our innocence, our values
Feeling devalued, abused, unclean, diseased

Disruptions can be passing or chronic
Once off or repeated
Taking us to dark places of the soul
Alone and unsupported
Silenced by demand or innuendo

Not knowing how to express the pain
Not knowing how to express the suffering
Or forced into silence to protect self
Hoping to keep safe from further harm
Silent frustration festering within, poisoning self

But if support is offered by caring souls
Silence can be lifted, a voice given
Relief comes with sharing of the pain
Cathartic telling of story
Finding a redemptive story of hope

Discovering ways to cope with the pain
Ways to be lifted out of the valley
Away from the shadow of death
With a lamp to light our path
Come beside still waters
To restore the soul*
*[*See Psalm 23]*

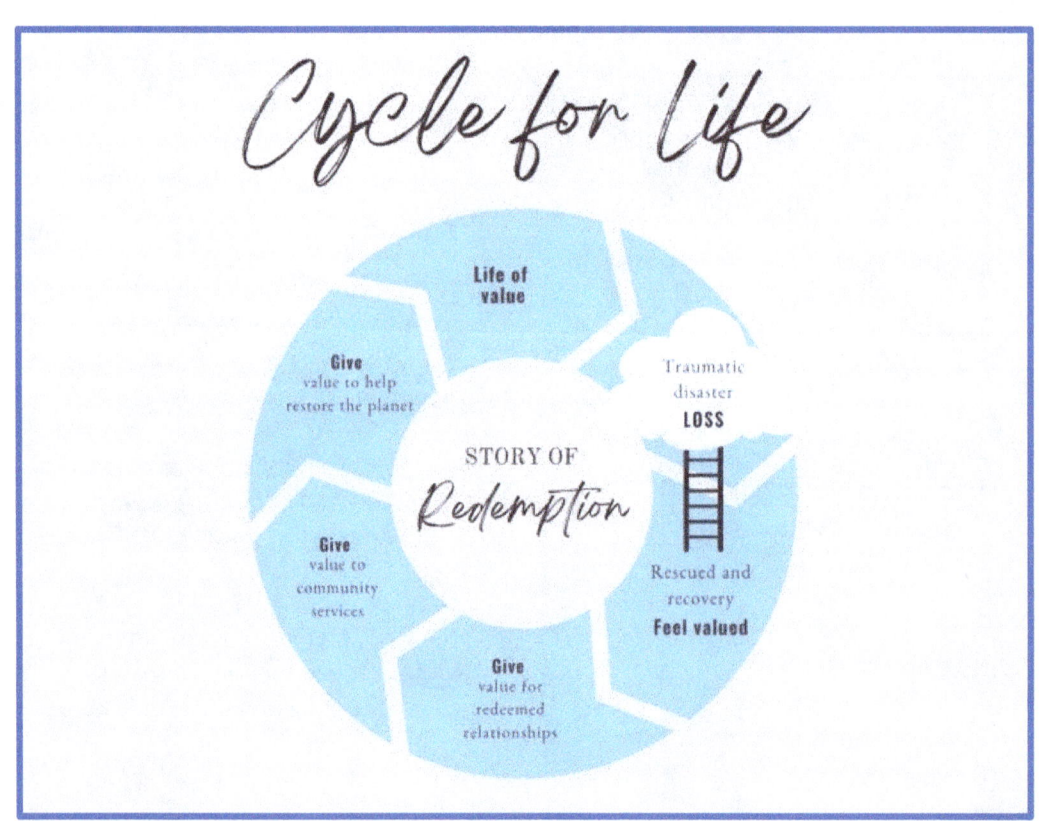

Figure 2: Cycle for life by Dr Julie Morsillo & Laura Boys,

Dr Julie Morsillo presentation trailer
Counselling after disasters seminar (2020)
www.youtube.com/watch?v=kBuH29ScVjg

Juliette finds courage
with redemptive stories

Poem by Dr Julie Morsillo PhD, 2015

Stories from own childhood experiences overcoming anxieties, growing up in Sutherland Shire, Sydney (late 1950s & 1960s).

1. Nervous yellow day
Juliette was nervous, such a yellow day, feeling down The stranger at the gate looked big and scary
*Take courage little one, don't worry, be happy
He has just come to bring us bread,* said Mummy.
She ate the bread to feed her tummy, very yummy.

2. Anxious blue day
Juliette was anxious, such a blue day
too hard to move day.
The swing grandpa made goes too high in the sky.
*Take courage small one, don't worry, be happy
Grandpa has made the rope so strong for you honey.*
She swung on the swing squealing,
enjoying flying high in the sky

3. Wary green day
Juliette was wary, such a green day,
feeling not so keen day.
The bush full of creepy stinging things like bull ants.
*Take courage sweet one, don't worry, be happy
The sap of this fern will soothe the pain my honey
So you can keep skipping in the sun, just for fun.*

4. Frightening black day
Juliette was frightened, such a black day, a too dark day
The water looked so cold, and dark and deep.
*Take courage cautious cousin, don't worry, be happy
The water will cool and calm you and buoy you up
Take the plunge to swim with the fishies in the sea.*

5. Scared red day
Juliette was scared, a red danger, take courage day
The tower was so dizzyingly high in the sky.
*Take courage careful sister, don't worry, be happy
The climb up will be worth the magnificent view
To see the land and sky from a bird's eye view.*

6. Shaking orange day
Juliette was shaking, a bright orange circus type day
School was far, walk down mountain,
punt across river, bus up hill.
*Take courage my child, don't worry, be happy
The adventure will be worth the journey
To play with more kids and toys than you ever did see*

7. Worried purple day
Juliette was worried, a purple challenging type day
The new home across the sea, away from friends & family
*Take courage young girl, don't worry, be happy
You will discover enchanting new people with story
More different and exciting than you have known.*

8. Wonderful rainbow day
Juliette was now no longer scared, a rainbow colour day
Discovering she liked new experiences, being free
Take courage she did, not worrying, being happy
Treasuring precious new people and places to see
A world full of wonder and laughter beyond imagination.

Worksheet A — Special story in life

Think about a special time in your life. This might be times like this:

Time with grand-parents as a child or

Time with family on a holiday or

Time of celebrating or

Time of regular rituals with food or festival

Prompts
This is a narrative therapy approach.
(see more in next section)
Talk about a special time in life,
to grow the positive redemptive story,
to help the *'thin'* story to be *'thickened'*,
to help find a story song to soar in life.

Questions
- Who was there?
- What did you see, hear, smell? What did you feel?
- When and how often did this happen?
- Where was this and why special?
- Why was this particularly enjoyable?

What is narrative Therapy?
by Alice Morgan (2000)
https://dulwichcentre.com.au/what-is-narrative-therapy/

Write a short story *of a special treasured time in life, to strengthen the positive hopeful stories in your life*

Dr Julie Morsillo interview
What is community psychology? (2014)
www.youtube.com/watch?v=kBuH29ScVjg

Part 1 – Stories of personal meaning in life

1.1 Care of own soul and body

What restores your soul? Tough times come in life, from national disasters adversely affecting whole communities, to personal ill-health issues, to trauma and grief, with loss of life's expectations and loss of those close to us. This can cause terrible suffering and distress, when our **souls feel broken and need restoring**.

Working hard daily, to be the best person you can be, to contribute to your families and support your friends and colleagues in the community can become overwhelming. Constantly **giving to others**, to fill their souls, as your role may demand, and you feel called to do. As humane people wanting to be compassionate, we use our gifts and skills to support others, especially those in need.

However, sometimes we promote hard work to the point of making our whole lives about work, with a good work ethic as worthwhile people, to the point of detriment to our own wellbeing. Living out our teachings, to always do as we are told by our elders, by our parents and by our work bosses, can became overwhelming. For those with children in the home, there is another layer of constant serving, not only to parents and bosses, but also a partner and our children. So can continually placing our children before our own needs.

Is this a sustainable way to live, to just give and give to others, in an endless roller-coaster? If our whole life is spent working hard for others, with no time for ourselves, we can become overtired, discouraged, always feeling so exhausted. This can lead to having nothing left to give, becoming unwell, physically and emotionally. Sometimes even losing faith in humanity. A place that can lead to burnout with **compassion fatigue.**

How can you restore your own soul to keep on giving? Even the strongest person, even the most mature person, needs time to restore their own soul.

What restores your soul, to give you a song to soar?

To restore my soul, I like to:
– Walking in the local parklands every day (see poem over page)
– Spend time in my garden
– Meet with family, friends, mentors and colleagues
– Swimming and water aerobics
– Playing the piano and singing in church
– Time with my grand-daughter
– Travelling to beautiful places with historical value and with natural beauty . . .

What helps to restore your soul?

Walk in the park
Poem by Dr Julie Morsillo, 2024

Walking in the park
Time to breath in
The beauty of nature
Stepping through time
To a garden of calm

Morning rays of sparkling sun
Peeking through the trees
Long shadows on the path
Of dreams during the night
Coming to haunt and taunt

Soothed by the fresh breeze
Rustling leaves in the bushes
Whisper comforting murmurs
Green trees reaching upwards, tall
Towards the wide blue sky

Birds flitter and flutter high in trees
Twittering and squawking of hope
Chattering to each other
Of better days and fun times
Laughing at worriers on the ground

Birds rise above the trees
Flying, soaring upwards
Above the troubles of daily life
To ride on the wind, effortlessly
Up, up and away

A garden seat to rest when tired
A swing to rock away the pain
A pond with water to cool
To cool the heated brow
Calm the troubled soul #

Worksheet B — Calm the Soul

Visualise a favourite place where you feel safe and calm

_____

*This place could be a place of **natural beauty**, like:*

Beach

River

Mountain

*Or a place of **safety**, like:*

Cave

Secluded place

Retreat

_____

Create a visual of this place
with a printed photo or drawing
or photo on phone or iPad
as an anchor to help stay calm

Prompts to begin
Start with a simple breathing exercise:
Slowly breath in and out, in and out, to begin to calm.
Roll your shoulders, clench and unclench your hands.
Close eyes if comfortable with that.
Think of a positive place,
with *no negative connotation*.

Question examples
- Who were you with, or who told you of this place?
- What makes this place so calming?
- When have you gone to such a place?
- Where is this place exactly, what happened there?
- Why is that place so calming?

Follow up
You can come back to this place anytime,
in your imagination, to calm yourself.
Maybe use this during counselling
if any triggering, to calm again.
You can use this at home to calm too.

Alternative Anchors to the Breath video
Trauma-Sensitive Mindfulness by David Treleaven (2021)
www.youtube.com/watch?v=C4YUs2OC-LQ

. Using anchors to calm website
Blue Knot Foundation:
Empowering recovery from complex trauma
https://blueknot.org.au/survivors/survivor-self-care/using-anchors/#:~:text=The%20place%20you%20choose%20doesn,a%20hospital%20or%20health%20centre

Care of physical body

The World Health Organization (WHO) definition of self-care:

Self-care refers to activities that individuals, families and communities undertake with the intention of enhancing health, preventing disease, limiting illness and restoring health. These activities are derived from knowledge and skills from the pool of both professional and lay experience. They are undertaken by lay people on their own behalf either separately or in participative collaboration with professionals. Seeking professional advice in self-care is part of the continuum of trying to maintain good health and prevent disease.

Our physical body is a temple, a sacred place, that requires reverence and care, in order to 'sing' well and 'soar'. The human body is made with intricate inter-related systems that work together mostly in harmony, if treated well. The incredible body, formed from the DNA of our parents coming together, who in turn received this from their parents, and so on, back to our ancestors. A creation born out of generations and generations of our ancestors, of those who have gone before us. This body is so precious, as this physical body is the one body we have all our lives. So great care is needed to keep it running well for our whole lifetime.

Like a vehicle for transport, say a car or a bike, to get us from place to place, so is our physical body. If a vehicle is not cared for well, if it becomes battered and bruised, with everyday wear and tear, and from any accidents, we can trade it in for another one.

But, imagine if you only could have one vehicle to use, car or bike, that had to last all your life. You could never exchange it, trade it in, or upgrade it, for a better model. How well would you look after that car or bike? Regular check-ups, cleaning, fixing something that does not sound right, or stops working properly. New tyres when the tread wears low. Watch for that engine light that goes on for a car. Check the safety light on the bike. Drive extra carefully, to not create too much wear and tear too quickly. Watch extra carefully for when the fuel gauge is close to empty to refill it. Being careful not to ignore any signs that the vehicle is breaking down or not working at its optimum.

So, extra care and respect is required for our own **physical body**, as our vehicle to take us from place to place. This special vehicle, of our physical body, has to **last a lifetime**. Thus, listening to our bodies to figure out what it is trying to tell us, and how we will respond, is vital. Not just ignoring a dull pain or sharp pain, or ignoring the fatigue, to soldier on, to push through. Pushing our bodies to perform at maximin. Carrying on our work, our duties, our responsibilities, even when our body is screaming with pain or yelling: *'Stop, I am exhausted'*. The more we push our bodies beyond reasonable limits, the more wear and tear is inflicted, often causing more pain for perhaps more long-lasting injuries of chronic problems, that can also come back to haunt us with age.

Our body need's **constant care**, so it can continue to be our vehicle to travel from place to place and do the many tasks we require it to do. Feeding our bodies with good food and drink, and also feeding our minds with good thoughts, good creative times and good reflective times to relax and refuel, ready to face the world. Filling our own tanks, so we have the capacity to cope with the challenges of life, and hopefully to support others in their life journey too.

Healthy eating and drinking, with plenty of water for hydration, and fresh wholesome foods, with lots of fruit and vegetables, a balanced diet, to support our body to work well. **Regular movement** of the body, with walking being so good for the body, or running or any kind of sport. Swimming is such a healthy and gentle exercise, with far less likelihood of injury, as the water cushions the body. Exercise to strengthen the core of our body can be so beneficial, like tai chi, yoga and pilates. Plus of course, dancing of any kind.

Plenty of rest with a long deep sleep at night, to restore the body physically and emotionally. Most of us need about 7 - 8 hours sleep at night, to feel refreshed in the morning. Over-tiredness can lead to feeling overwhelmed with the challenges of life, to become depressed, or very grumpy with the people around us, adversely affecting our work and our relationships.

To help with a good night's sleep, **sleep hygiene** can be a strategy. This can involve making sure we have some relaxed time before trying to go to sleep. Perhaps listening to calming music or meditation app, or reading a novel. For some, watching TV or reading online, although the strong light can be too stimulating for some.

If you tend to constantly worry about work and life, like a broken record in your head, as we all do at times, then try setting aside a special time to worry, well before the relaxing time leading up to bed-time. This *'worry time'* is to think through the problem to define it clearly, and perhaps write it down. Then come up with an option to two to cope with the problem, ready to put it aside for a while. The solution to your problem, could be an easy temporary one, such as, *'It is no use worrying about this, as that is not going to help, and besides I can't do anything about this now, so I will stop worrying for now, and leave it until the morning.'*

Then set aside a **time to relax** before trying to sleep. This could be listening to relaxing music or reading something relaxing, as above.

(Dr David Morawetz, 2000, Sleep better without drugs)

If you think you are worrying about something you can't do anything about, it might be worth remembering the Serenity prayer:

> ### SERENITY PRAYER
> God grant me the serenity
> to **accept** the things I cannot change
> **courage** to change the things I can
> and the **wisdom** to know the difference.

Care of your own soul, where you spend time engaging your mind with life-giving thoughts and actions that feed your inner self, with fuel to face the challenges of life.

Times to reflect on life, with mindfulness, or an attitude of prayer. Not just prayers of supplication, but prayers of gratitude for the blessings we do have in life. For the blessing of life itself. Some do this in groups in the form of Sunday worship or a bible study or prayer group, to be reflective as a faith community. Others do this with a support group of friends or with others with similar needs. Yet others do this with family or extended family, as a weekly ritual or celebrations of special times.

Care of the soul can often involve the creative arts, fine arts, crafts and music. Creating works of art, or sewing or needlework to create beautiful things, or make something beautiful or practical with wood or clay or stone or whatever. For many, listening or creating music that soothes or inspires the soul. Music can be so emotive, to bring joy or bitter-sweet memories.

Time being immersed in restorative nature, from gardening to walking in nature-filled parklands, with the natural beauty and fresh air, can feed the soul too.

Serenity Prayer origins
https://uscatholic.org/news_item/commentary-how-i-discovered-i-was-wrong-about-the-origin-of-the-serenity-prayer/

Worksheet C — Relaxed Movement

What gentle relaxed movements can you build into your weekly routine? For example, you could consider:

_____

Walking in parklands

Running or riding in parklands

Dancing exercise

Tai Chi, Pilates of Yoga

Swimming or water aerobics

_____

Movement can improve your sense of wellbeing, to soar in life

Prompts
Think of a time when you were happy or not so sad. Think of any movements you have done in the past as a child, or maybe something new, such as:
- Walking, bushwalking, running or skipping
- Riding a bike, alone or with friends
- Playing a team sport
- Swimming in a pool or at the beach
- Fishing, snorkelling, kayaking or boating
- Gym or home exercise workout
- Dancing classes or dancing for fun
- Gardening

Morning stretches: Move it or Lose it Australia
by Stephanie Smilas (2019)
www.youtube.com/watch?v=u737fA2JWnY

Practice one or more of these activities two or three times a week. RECORD day and time

Monday--

Tuesday--

Wednesday--

Thursday---

Friday---

Saturday---

Sunday---

1.2 Positive Psychology and wellbeing

Personal skills, values, and supports
Positive Psychology concept by Prof Martin Seligman

Positive Psychology is grounded in the belief that people want to lead meaningful and fulfilling lives, to cultivate what is best within them, and to enhance their experiences of love, work, and play (Positive Psychology Center, 2016). Creating your own song to sing in life.

pos'itive [poz-i-tiv] a. constructive in intention or attitude; showing optimism and confidence; measured or moving forward or in a direction of improvement or progress n. a good, affirmative, or constructive quality or attribute

psychol'ogy [sahy-kol-uh-jee] n. the study of the mind and behavioural characteristics typical of an individual or group in relation to a particular field of knowledge or activity

Positive Psychology is the scientific study of human flourishing, and an applied approach to optimal functioning. It has also been defined as the study of the strengths and virtues that enable individuals, communities and organisations to thrive (Gable & Haidt, 2005).

Prof Martin Seligman, American Psychological Association President in the late 1990s, suggested that psychology turn toward understanding and building human strengths to complement the traditional emphasis on healing damage. Psychology had often neglected the positive side of life, having spent so much time primarily concerned with the psychopathology, of finding and naming each life problem. As a result, psychologists and psychiatrists have managed to measure with considerable precision, and effectively treat, a number of major mental illnesses. However, this progress came at a cost. Relieving life's miseries made building the states that make life worth living less of a priority (Seligman, 2002).

Prof Martin Seligman developed the concept of positive psychology, to **build up a person's identity**, as an antidote to the traditional psychotherapy approaches, and the more recent popular cognitive and behavioural therapies.

Psychotherapy tends to delve into the problems of the past to resolve those issues. This can be very helpful for many. However, sometimes it can be overwhelming, with some finding staying in the present more helpful in order to move forward.

Cognitive and behavioural psychology approaches, on the other hand, deals with the present problems within and in our relationships. This too can be very helpful. However, this approach can place immense pressure on some that they have to change this re-enforcing those negative cognitions. For those an acceptance approach can work better.

Having a psychotherapist or a CBT therapist, to listen to all your problems, empathetically, and validate your thoughts, feeling and responses, and showing you the reasons why you think and feel like that, can feel good, and even be helpful. But for some, it can be become overwhelming to only think of the problems.

Positive psychology, on the other hand, starts with the **positive aspects of your life**, both within your own identity and skill-set, to build up your self-identity, as well as to notice what supports you have, or could reach out for, to support you in your daily life. By building up your inner thought life in positive ways, for a more resilient person, can then help to deal with the problems in your life, with a more positive mindset.

Also, positive psychology offers ideas of positive **creative ways forward**, including doing creative projects, and finding time to relax and enjoy life with friends or in nature. This more relaxed state can help with positive and calm responses to the problematic issues that arise in life, with a sense of personal agency, feeling competent and able to cope well. **Giving a song in life to soar.**

Mindfulness and gratitude

Positive psychology also uses **mindfulness** techniques, to stay in the moment, and enjoy the moment, so as not to endlessly feel guilty or sad about the past and get depressed, or anxiously worrying about what might happen in the future. So to have a more calm mind and calm responses to life issues and problems.

Positive psychology encourages **gratitude** for what you do have or have had and can have in the future. Like, keeping a gratitude diary, as a way to focus on the positive, recording one to three things a day to be grateful for. Research has shown that this helps to create a positive mindset to become a more hopeful person, who values themselves and what they can offer, and then in turn can values others and what they can give as well, helping create respectful relationships.

Time in nature, can help with gratitude, by simply walking in nature or gardening to create a nature space, with more connectedness to land and country, like our Indigenous cultures have so carefully done over millennia past. Time to relax and breathe in fresh air in parklands and in the bush, away from the fast-paced modern life. To calm our bodies and calm our souls.

Prof Martin Seligman, the father of positive psychology, has more recently developed a schema called PERMA™:

- **Positive emotion** – like hope, interest, joy, love, compassion, pride, amusement and gratitude
- **Engagement** – living in the present moment, focused on the task at hand
- **Relationships** – feeling supported, loved and valued by others
- **Meaning** – sense of belonging and purpose, serving something greater than ourselves
- **Accomplishments** – working towards and reaching goals with perseverance for mastery and competence

All positive psychology concepts to build upon in life, for a meaningful and fulfilling life.
Giving a song in life to soar.

"The aim of Positive Psychology is to catalyze a change in psychology from a preoccupation only with repairing the worst things in life to also building the best qualities in life."
- Martin Seligman.

Prof Martin Seligman article
Seligman, M. (2018). PERMA and the building blocks of well-being. *The Journal of Positive Psychology*. 13 (4).

Prof Martin Seligman book
Seligman M. E. P. (1991). *Learned optimism: How to change your mind and your life*. A.A. Knopf.

Prof Martin Seligman lecture
The new era on positive psychology Ted Talk (2008)
www.ted.com/talks/martin_seligman_the_new_era_of_positive_psychology?trigger=5s

Prof Martin Seligman lecture
Flourishing – a new understanding of wellbeing (2012)
www.youtube.com/watch?v=e0LbwEVnfJA

Prof Shelly Gable & Prof Jonathan Haidt article
Gable, S.L. & Haidt, J. (2005) What (and why) is positive psychology? Review of General Psychology, 9,2, 103-110.

Worksheet D — Inspiring Music

Music can be very emotive. Choose a piece of music that has been inspiring or relaxing for you. It could be:

_____

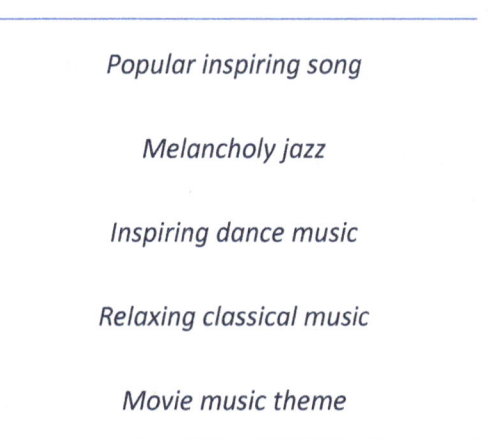

Popular inspiring song

Melancholy jazz

Inspiring dance music

Relaxing classical music

Movie music theme

_____

Prompts
Music can bring back good memories.
Music can be inspiring to think more positively.
Music can be relaxing to decrease stress levels.
So what music inspires or relaxes you?

Listen to the music together and talk about how and when this music inspired or relaxed you..
This music can be played when feeling distressed, to booster your mood and help find a song to soar.

Play the musical piece.
Write out the words
or images it conjures up.

When has this music inspired or soothed you?

Worksheet inspired by a workshop in Melbourne 2008, led by Angel Yuen, narrative therapist from Canada.

Angel Yuen talk
Co-discovering hope with children facing hardships (2021)
www.youtube.com/watch?v=eo7RwdfVtV4

Angel Yuen book
Yuen, A. (2019). *Pathways beyond despair: Re-authoring lives of young people through narrative therapy.* Dulwich Centre Publications

For more commentary on the use of music in therapy
Australian Music Therapy Association (2024)
www.austmta.org.au/about-us/what-is-mt/

Music Therapy overview video
Music Therapy in Australia & New Zealand video (2013)
www.youtube.com/watch?v=4pCEBKxec8w

Music Therapy Impact Insight Series - Benj
Nordoff-Robbins Music Therapy Australia (2018)
www.youtube.com/watch?v=3i41HswYLQU

Personal, relational and collective wellbeing
Wellbeing values concept by Prof Isaac Prilleltensky

Personal well-being
At a personal level, we need to feel **appreciated**, and that we are valued and cared for by others, and have personal agency, with a sense of control over our own lives, having a voice with choice, to freely make choices that suit us, without any coercive control or threats by others.

Relational well-being
At a relational level to have **respectful** relationships around us, that are dignified, with fair participation, to feel valued, accepted and supported.

Collective well-being
At a community level to have appropriate, fair and equitable community services for **adequate** education and healthcare, and housing that is safe and well supported.

So all three levels of well-being are needed for you to develop your **own song to sing in life, to soar.**

Prof Geoffrey Nelson & Prof Isaac Prilleltensky book
Nelson, G. B., & Prilleltensky, I. (2005). *Community psychology: In pursuit of liberation and well-being*. Palgrave Macmillan.

Prof Isaac Prilleltensky & Dr Ora Prilleltensky book
Prilleltensky, I., & Prilleltensky, O. (2007). *Promoting Well-Being: Linking Personal, Organizational, and Community Change*. John Whiley & Sons.

Prof Isaac Prilleltensky Ted Talk
Community Wellbeing: Socialize or social lies (2010)
www.youtube.com/watch?v=WJlx8CI-rRg

Prof Isaac Prilleltensky presentation
Mattering, Happiness, and Wellbeing (2024)
www.youtube.com/watch?v=iluUHZnjMsw

Figure 1: Finding redemptive stories by Dr Julie Morsillo

Physical and emotional safety

Hierarchy of needs concept by Prof Abraham Maslow

Maslow argued that basic survival needs, such as food, shelter, and rest, along with personal safety needs, must be satisfied before the individual can satisfy the higher psychological needs of having caring relationships and feeling valued, in order to work towards achieving one's potential in life (Maslow, 1943). To sing one's own song in life, to soar.

Prof Abraham Maslow lecture
Further reaches of human nature (1967)
www.youtube.com/watch?v=pagvjnTEEvg

Prof Abraham Maslow article
Maslow, A.H. (1943). Theory of Human Motivation. *Psychological Review*, Vol 50, p. 370-396.

5. Self-actualisation – reached potential

4. Esteem – respected, sense of achievement

3. Social - feeling valued by friends
↑
2. Safety needs – security, resources & safety
↑
1. Basic needs to survive –food, water, shelter, rest

Abraham Maslow's Hierarchy of Needs

Personal empowerment

Empowerment stories by Prof Julian Rappaport

Personal empowerment, is moving from *'learned helplessness'* (Martin Seligman, 1991), to a sense of power and control, of personal agency with a sense of empowerment, so that you feel you have a say in life and can take some control over your own life (Rappaport, 2020).

To feel like you have your own melodious song to sing in life, not just singing in someone else's choir.

personal agency   confidence   knowledge
strategy   leadership   responsibility
growth   advice   mentor   coach

EMPOWERMENT

Motivate   succeed   competence   educated
develop   improve   enable   guidance
communication   spiritual   negotiation

Audio of an empowerment article
Empowerment on Julian Rappaport concepts (2018)
www.youtube.com/watch?v=yrimm5JScQY

Prof Julian Rappaport article
Rappaport, J. (1995) Empowerment meets narrative: Listening to stories and creating settings. *American Journal of Community Psychology;* Oct 1995; 23, 5

Lack of empowerment story
Story of Hagar

This poignant bible story of Hagar, shows her dis-empowered position, as an Egyptian slave of Abraham and Sarah. Hagar's body was used to produce a child for them. But when old Sarah, finally was having a child of her own, then Hagar and her child were treated badly. She escaped for a while to the desert. A tough life.

As the feminist theologian Prof Phyllis Trible, says in Texts of Terror (1984):

"**Hagar is a symbol of the oppressed.**
She becomes many things to many people, all sorts of rejected women find their stories in her.

Hagar is the faithful maid exploited,
the black woman used by the male and abided by the female of the ruling class,
the surrogate mother, the resident alien without legal recourse, the other woman,
the runaway youth,
the religious fleeing from affliction,
the pregnant young woman alone,
the expelled wife, the homeless woman,
the indignant relying upon handouts from the power structure, the welfare mother,
and the self-effecting female whose own identity shrinks in service to others."

A story for those who are oppressed,
with no voice, who are dis-empowered,
and no song to sing for their life.

Prof Phyllis Trible in Texts of terror
Trible, P. (1984). *Texts of terror: Literary-feminist readings of Biblical narratives.* Fortress Press.

See commentary on empowering whose who are oppressed in the community

Prof Julian Rappaport article
Begins with this story of Hagar and explores ways to empower and bring joy to oppressed
Rappaport, J. (2000). **Community narratives: Tales of terror and joy.** *American Journal of Community Psychology,* 28, p.1-24.

See also:
Prof Shawn Ginwright article
Healing centered engagement
shifting from trauma-informed care
Ginwright, S. (2018). The future of healing: Shifting from trauma informed care to healing centered engagement. https://ginwright.medium.com/the-future-of-healing-shifting-from-trauma-informed-care-to-healing-centered-engagement-634f557ce69c

Prof Shawn Ginwright interview
www.youtube.com/watch?v=GKItZaF6Wb0

Worksheet E — Empowerment story

Think of some aspect of your life where you feel stuck or trapped or resentful with little control or empowerment, such as:

_____

Feel disrespected at home

Feel stuck in job

Asked to do too much

Overtired by workload

Can't say NO to requests
_____

Prompts
Talk about a difficult issue or conflict in daily life
What it is like, if feeling overwhelmed (disempowered), trapped or unable to control or resolve the issue?
What is your usual response to the issue?
Now think of time when could respond differently or resist, standing up for yourself better.

Resilience questions
- What was your unique or different response?
- How is this better (or worse)?
- What might be the best response?
- How can we practice this best response?

Can you think of a time when you did have some control or perhaps could change your response for more control? Perhaps:

_____

Able to gain some respect at home

Negotiate about job

Take some time to relax

Take some time for fun

Say NO to requests
_____

Narrative Therapy:
Acts of resistance & acts of reclaiming
Presentation by Loretta Pederson (2018)
www.youtube.com/watch?v=ftCAmkYnAY4

Angel Yuen article on responses to trauma
Yuen, A. (2009). Less pain, more gain: Explorations of responses verses effects when working with the consequences of trauma. *Explorations: An E-Journal of Narrative Practice*, 2, 6-16. Dulwich Centre Publications.

Narrative Therapy:
Surviving the ocean of depression
Tips for survival from refugees in Adelaide
https://dulwichcentre.com.au/part-2-surviving-the-ocean-of-depression/

1.3 Personal meaning in life

Power of meaning
Concept by Dr Emily E. Smith in Power of meaning

What makes people happy? This is the question *Emily Smith (2017),* had as a journalist, embarking on her PhD research. She imagined she might find that happiness could be found in having a well-paid job, a permanent home, for a comfortable life, with a satisfying intimate relationship. However, in her reading of philosophers, psychiatrists *(including Victor Frankl below)*, psychologists, and revered religious figures, as well as interviews with many people from all walks of life, she was surprised to find in that they were searching, not for happiness, but for meaning in life. Their own song to soar.

Dr Emily E. Smith's **four pillars of meaning**:

1. Belonging – A sense of belonging to a community was all important. Satisfying and respectful relationships with family and friends, partners, colleagues and even strangers, were valued.

2. Purpose – Reflecting our values and wanting to serve for the greater good of others in the local or broader world. *Researcher Adam Grant has found that professions focused on helping others—teachers, surgeons, clergy, and therapists—all tend to rate their jobs as more meaningful, and that people who imbue their work with purpose are more dedicated to their jobs. Having purpose has also been tied to many positive outcomes, including increased learning for students in school and better health.*

3. Redemptive life stories – People who describe their lives as meaningful, tend to have a strong identity story, where they overcome tough times of suffering, learning how to grow from the experiences with a sense of personal agency and support from others, for a new hopeful redemptive story.

Dr Emily E Smith presentation
The power of meaning: Crafting a life that matters (2018)
www.youtube.com/watch?v=9bVl4xdPUns

Dr Emily E Smith book
Smith, E.E. (2017). *The power of meaning: Finding fulfilment in a world obsessed with happiness.* Penguin.

4. Transcendence – Experiences in life that fill us with a sense of awe and wonder. This can be religious or spiritual experiences alone or with others, or immersing ourselves in nature. These experiences can help us to decrease our own self-focus, to engage in more generous, helpful behaviours. So less self-importance, and more of a sense of meaning or place in the world.

> The meaning of life, is to give life meaning
> – Viktor Frankl

Logotherapy
Concept by Dr Viktor Frankl

Dr Viktor Frankl, talks about the importance of **finding meaning and purpose** in life. As a psychiatrist, who had survived a German concentration camp, where hope was hard to find, he developed this theory of **logotherapy**. He states that we need to find meaning in life, through **inspiring creative projects**, or in **giving to others in meaningful ways,** with acts of kindness, being compassionate, or adding to the knowledge of the world. He realised the importance of creating and of giving, to sustain yourself, even if you lose your family, as he did. He found some meaning in life, by learning to give to others and support them through terrible times and the good times, too.

Quotes from Dr Viktor Frankl's book
– Man's search for meaning (1950)
of his time in a concentration camp:

"The majority of prisoners suffered from a kind of inferiority complex. We all had once been or had fancied ourselves to be 'somebody.' Now we were treated like complete nonentities. *(The conscious-ness of one's inner value is anchored in higher, more spiritual things, and cannot be shaken by camp life. But how many free men, let alone prisoners, possess it?)* Without consciously thinking about it, the average prisoner felt himself utterly degraded . . . Human life, under any circumstances, never ceases to have a meaning, and that this infinite meaning of life includes suffering and dying, privation and death."

Our lives are a treasure, because they are finite, with a limited time on this earth, to develop your own **song to sing so we can soar in life.**

Worksheet F – Meaning in Life

Where do you find meaning, sense of belonging or purpose in your life? This could be in a:

_____

- Meaningful role at home
- Meaningful role in job
- Meaningful volunteer work
- Creative project
- Creative craft
- Woodwork or metalwork project
- Creating music or art

_____

Prompts
Think of a time in the past, when doing something:
– Meaningful or with a purpose - like helping a family
   member, friend, neighbour or colleague
– Creative craft, art or music for home or gift
– Performing artistic or musical skills
– Volunteering to help those in need

Consider doing more meaningful things, like bringing back art or music into your life, to inspire or calm or feel like you are creating a metaphorical or actual song to sing in life to soar.

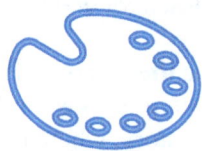

Finding meaning in life talk
Let's talk about mental health podcast (2024)
www.youtube.com/watch?v=3QPw57KlF1U

Dr Emily E Smith presentation on meaning in life
How to build four pillars of meaning for flourishing life (2022)
www.youtube.com/watch?v=9bVl4xdPUns

Grandpa's bush hideaway

Poem by Dr Julie Morsillo
and mother, Shirley Mitchell, 2015

Based on childhood memories in late 50s and early 60s of paternal Grandpa Ralph Mitchell & Grandma Sarah Mitchell (née Wheat) in their bush home, next door to us for a while, in Illawong (Aboriginal name meaning between two waters), Sutherland Shire, Sydney.

1. *Little house*
Grandpapa, your bush house is so small
But I can't find the toilet at all
Look what we have instead
The little house down the back, Grandpa said
Bull-ants are big with a nasty bite
So make sure you look both left and right

2. *Bath tub*
Grandpapa your bush house is so small
But I can't find the bathroom at all
We bath in the tub as water's no lack
We watch out for spiders with red on their back
We always close the door up tight
We don't want Grandma to get a fright

3. *Food*
Grandpapa your bush house is so far from the store
When food runs out, how do you get more?
Tomatoes, beans, and berries I grew
I use them to make my Mitchell Stew
Flowers I planted for beauty too
Bees and butterflies in they flew

4. *Swings*
Grandpapa your bush house is so small
I can't find any toys at all
Look out in the yard and you will see
I made a swing in the large gum tree
With bent boughs, nails, rope and string
Made us all a wonderful swing

5. *Kookaburra*
Grand-papa your bush house is so small
There is no room for pets at all
Let's put out small pieces of steak
For wild kookaburras to take
Kookaburra laughed to see such fun
And swooped on down to take each one

6. *Music*
Grand-papa your bush house is so small
There is no player for music at all
Here's a small pedal organ for grandma to play
And grand-father clock that strikes each day
Music draws the family in
When we gather round the organ to sing

7. *Story*
Grandpapa your bush house is so small
What will we do when night-time falls?
There are stories to tell how I came to harm
Gunshot in my thumb, shrapnel in my arm
Saw my mates die at Gallipoli's shore
Let's pray for peace, never honouring war

8. *Door knocking*
Grandpapa your bush house is so small
Do you ever visit other homes at all?
I love my neighbour and the poor
So I go knocking from door to door
Jesus's love can bring us peace
Only love can cause wars to cease

9. *God's creation*
Grandpapa your bush house is so small
Do you ever wish that you had more?
I've peace in my heart, God's given to me
We have all of earth's creation to enjoy
There is a whole universe out there to explore
We pray too, each day how we can share more.

Painting by Shirely Mitchell (nee Risk, my mother)

1.4 Gratitude journal

Mattering - Feeling valued to give value
Concept by Prof Isaac Prilleltensky

We need to feel valued by others, that we matter, in order to be able to give back value to others. Caring for others in our lives, calmly and kindly, letting them know they are valued, calling them out at their best, with affirmations, so they feel appreciated and in turn might be able to appreciate and value others.

But firm boundaries are needed, so when others are disrespectful and unkind, saying firmly and calmly, **no**, that behaviour is not good enough: *I respect you and you need to respect me. We are both valuable and need to be treated as such.*

Prof Isaac Prilleltensky article
Prilleltensky, I. (2014). Meaning-making, mattering, and thriving in community psychology: From co-optation to amelioration and transformation. *Psychosocial Intervention,* 23(2) p.151-154.

> NOTE: **WRITE DISTRESSING STORY FIRST idea**
>
> Those feeling very distressed about life, can be encouraged to **write out the story of distress and heartache first,** perhaps over a few days or a week. This way, the overwhelming negative story has a chance to come out, rather than just staying in the mind, like a broken record playing over the over.
>
> Once that negative distressing story is released and acknowledged, out on paper, then can move on to **starting a gratitude journal**. This can help recall any positive stories from the past, when felt valued, with the **more hopeful stories to sing.** Plus with the negative released, the mind has a chance to recall the positive, *counting our blessings,* and to be able **to see current positive things in life, and be open to new positive experiences to soar in life.**

Mindfulness with gratitude journal

A **mindfulness** attitude is one of being aware of the positive, hopeful **life-giving** things in our lives. We often take for granted. or gloss over the positive things, since we are so often caught up in our problem story. We can feel discouraged and depressed about the past, or anxious about the future, so not appreciating the present moment, any blessings or small things we can be **grateful for**.

Keeping a daily gratitude journal, can help to notice the positive aspects of life, rather than constantly thinking of the problems or potential problems. Keeping a gratitude journal can lead to a more positive optimistic attitude to life in general, and towards others.

Gratitude helps develop your own song to soar.

How to practice gratitude
Mindful: Healthy mind, healthy life (2024)
www.mindful.org/an-introduction-to-mindful-gratitude/

Caron Baginski presentation
How to start a gratitude journal
www.youtube.com/watch?v=GZghu_xFRM8

Dr Katherine Thompson book
Thompson, K. (2020*). Christ-centred mindfulness: Connection to self and God.* Acorn Press.

Worksheet G – Gratitude Journal

Think of three different things that you can be grateful for, on a particular day. This could be:

RECORD what you are grateful for each day. You *could start your own gratitude journal.*

Someone who loves you

Something you enjoy doing

Something in nature you like

Something you can create

A place you like to visit

Gratitude journal prompts
Positive experiences, people, places, and times in nature, that you might be grateful for on a particular day, such as:

- Best part of the day
- Best gift or support received
- Best gift or support given
- Something you enjoyed doing
- Something you enjoyed making
- Something that made you smile
- Someone who made you feel loved
- Someone who made you laugh
- Animal or plant you are grateful for
- Appreciating nature in some way
- Enjoying the great outdoors some way

Monday----------------------------

Tuesday---------------------------

Wednesday-------------------------

Thursday--------------------------

Friday----------------------------

Saturday--------------------------

Sunday----------------------------

Granny Jane is stolen

*Poem by Dr Julie Morsillo
& mother Shirley Mitchell, 2016*

My great-great-great Granny Jane
Found herself hungry once again
Cold grey damp days all the same
No family to turn to, no-one came
T'was sad lonely old London Town
Granny Jane cried, what will I do?
No-one to help me. Just have to make do!

Back then Granny Jane was still young
She and her friends still wanted some fun
They were poor as church mice, ho-hum
What could they do to get out in the sun
Come up with a plan so we can run
Granny Jane cried, what will I do?
No-one to help me. Just have to make do!

Let's steal from the rich to give to us poor
Let's go knocking on a door
Girls eyed a rich looking man they saw
Come with us for a fun you'll adore
While he was distracted all agog
Cheeky girls stole his wallet and watch
Granny Jane cried, what will I do?
No-one to help me. Just have to make do!

The plan you know was not so well handled
Man screamed blue murder and commanded
Police come and catch this wrench! Surrender!
Jane ran, tripped over and landed
Poor Granny Jane was caught red handed
Granny Jane cried, what will I do?
No-one to help me, Just have to make do!

Granny Jane was hauled into the court
Judge looked at her up and down with thought
Heard the man's complaint being brought
She stole my money, he was wrought
No-one gave Granny Jane a second thought
Just a poor girl who had been caught
Granny Jane cried, what will I do?
No-one to help me, Just have to make do!

She can't be trusted, she is beyond the pail
Judge ordered her to go straight to jail
Jails all full, so we'll send her away
We'll steal her from her homeland today
On a convict ship to sail away
To teach her not to steal from a male
Granny Jane cried, what will I do?
No-one to help me. Just have to make do!

Jane forced on convict ship, Surprize
Slave to the owner, in terrible guise
Cold dark smelly, with rats to despise
Endless seas with rocking and seasickness
Sadly, some of the girls just didn't survive
Granny Jane cried, what will I do?
No-one to help me. Just have to make do!

Finally enough of the sea so rough
Land was in sight, it was no bluff
But it all looked so bare as can be
Not many people but oh so much dust
Sunshine and warmth, it was good stuff
Granny Jane cried, what will I do?
No-one to help me. Just have to make do!

Jane knew to survive in the can
She would need to have herself a man
One to protect her from those with plans
Her only option was to find such a man
To love her and marry her if he can
Clever Granny Jane did find such a man
Granny Jane cried, what will I do?
No-one to help me. Just have to make do!

Slaves to tough masters, so deprived
Making them work so they nearly died
But at least gave them food to survive
Jane and her hubby knew to behave
After seven long year, free, still alive
Granny Jane cried, what will I do?
No-one to help me. Just have to make do!

Jane Ison with William, nine children did she bear
Sunshine for warmth, to play, swim and care
In the land with boundless plains to share
With family, a land that is girt by sea
An island home, far away from her heritage
Granny Jane cried, what will I do?
No-one to help me. Just have to make do!

Note: This poem is based on a paternal ancestor sent as a convict to Australia on the ship Surprize, part of second fleet of white colonisers.
--> Sculptures of convict women on Hobart's waterfront, Tasmania.

1.5 Finding meaning after loss

Grief
Quote by Jamie Anderson, 2022

"Grief, I've learned, is really love. It's all the love you want to give but cannot give. The more you loved someone, the more you grieve. All of that unspent love gathers up in the corners of your eyes and in that part of your chest that gets empty and hollow feeling. The happiness of love turns to sadness when unspent. **Grief is just love with no place to go**."

Learn from grief
Quote by Prof Michael Cholbi, 2022

"Grief is an opportunity for self-knowledge. Grieving is a very emotionally intense experience as we have lost something of value and care about.
We need to work out what we want to retain in the relationship with the deceased and what the relationship will look like.
We need to learn about our values, concerns and commitments."

Prof Michael Cholbi book
Cholbi, M. (2022). *Grief: A philosophical guide.* Princeton University Press.

Prof Michael Cholbi talk
Philosophy of grief
www.youtube.com/watch?v=PHmInLvrvIM

Finding meaning after grief and loss
Concept by Prof David Kessler

"Each person's grief is as unique as their fingerprint. But what everyone has in common is that no matter how they grieve, they share a need for their grief to be witnessed. That doesn't mean needing someone to try to lessen it or reframe it for them. The need is for someone to be fully present to the magnitude of their loss without trying to point out the silver lining." (Kessler, 2019)

Kessler gives readers a roadmap to **remembering** those who have died **with more love than pain**; he shows us how to move forward in a way that **honours our loved ones**. Kessler's insight is both professional and intensely personal. His journey with grief began when, as a 13 year old child, he witnessed a mass shooting at the same time his mother was dying. For most of his life, Kessler taught physicians, nurses, counsellors, police, and first responders about end of life, trauma, and grief, as well as leading talks and retreats for those experiencing grief. Despite his knowledge, his life was upended by the sudden death of his twenty-one-year-old son, causing much change in his life (Kessler, 2019).

Yet he finally **found meaning**, not in the death, but in the **legacy** left by his son, that had enriched his life, for a more fulfilling song in his life.

Prof David Kessler talk
How to heal from grief by changing your story (2023)
www.youtube.com/watch?v=YroTNH1lIvo

Prof David Kessler book
Kessler, D. (2019). *Finding meaning: The sixth stage of grief.* Ebury Publishing

Dr Elizabeth Kubler-Ross & Prof David Kessler article
Kübler-Ross, E., & Kessler, D. (2012). On grief and grieving: Finding the meaning of grief through the five stages of loss. Scribner.

Worksheet H — Meaning after Loss

Think of a distressing loss in your life. For example, this could be:

_____

Death of a loved one

Separation or divorce

Loss of a job

Loss of a home

Loss of a partnership

Loss of friends

Loss of good health

_____

Describe what you have learnt from loss and how you can memorialise this, such as:

_____

Legacy from loved one

Good memories

Ways of living

New skills or resilience

Ways to celebrate

A memorial

_____

Prompts to begin
Grief and loss can be heart-breaking:
loosing someone you have loved dearly,
being rejected by someone you love, or
loss of expectations in our relationships, and
loss of expectations of how life and health should be.

So hard to suffer from grief and loss.
But often we can learn something from it
to grow as a person, being more resilient to face
life challenges, and develop your own song to sing.

Prof David Kessler Ted Talk
How to find meaning after loss (2021)
www.youtube.com/watch?v=D3azoUEEy3E

1.6 Gratitude for hopeful life stories

The Psychological Self as Actor, Agent, and Author
Concept by Prof Dan P McAdams

Dan McAdam suggests that in life we grow from an actor, to agent to author of our own lives.

1. **Actor** – As a young child, we start by being like an actor in a play, following the lines and rules set by others (like singing in another's choir).
2. **Agent** – With a little more maturing in mid-childhood this changes to feeling more like an agent, with some fears, but also plans and goals for the future.
3. **Author** – As an emerging adult, this usually changes to feeling like the author of our own lives, where we realise we can make up our own song to sing in life.

Three level model of personality
Concept by Prof Dan P McAdams

McAdams three personality levels are:

1. **Dispositional traits**: a person's general tendencies. For example, the Big Five personality traits list: openness, conscientiousness, extraversion, agreeableness, neuroticism.

2. **Characteristic adaptation:** a person's desires, beliefs, concerns, and coping mechanisms.

3. **Life stories:** the stories that give a life a sense of unity, meaning, and purpose. This is known as narrative identity.

So developing the meaningful stories in life, or the redemptive stories in life, helps us to find out own song to sing in life and soar.

Feature	The self as . . .		
	Actor	Agent	Author
The self's contents	Social roles, skills, traits; social reputation	Personal goals, plans, values, hopes and fears	Life narrative
Mechanisms of self-definition	Self-attribution and categorization, built on observation of social performances	Exploration of and commitment to life projects; planning; prioritizing investments for future	Autobiographical reasoning; construction of an integrative life story
Temporal emphasis	Present	Present and future	Past, present, and future
Psychosocial problem	Self-regulation	Self-esteem	Self-continuity
Developmental emergence	Age 2–3: early childhood	Age 7–9: mid- to late childhood	Age 15–25: adolescence and emerging adulthood
Culture provides . . .	Performance norms, display rules; behavioral constraints	Scripts for goal content, timing, and goal pursuit/disengagement; motivational constraints	A menu of images, metaphors, and stories for life; narrative constraints

Table 1. Features of the Psychological Self

by Prof Dan McAdams, 2013

Prof Dan McAdams book
McAdams, D. P. (2006). *The redemptive self: Stories Americans live by.* Oxford University Press.

Prof Dan McAdams article
McAdams, D. (2013). The psychological self, as actor, agent and author. *Perspectives on Psychological Science*, May 2013. 8(3):272-295.

Prof Dan McAdams lecture
Narrative approaches to the self
www.youtube.com/watch?v=C1eEpK23Hvg

Prof Dan McAdams lecture
Narrative Identity & the constructed imagination
www.youtube.com/watch?v=h5noiP9VD4U

Can Grumpy Gum survive?

*Poem by Dr Julie Morsillo
& mother, Shirley Mitchell, 2012*

1. Tiny Gum tree is quaking with fear
OH NO! Great storm clouds are coming too near
This wind will blow me right over, just here
Nothing will be left of me, that is quite clear

2. Young Kooka flying by with laughter and song
DON'T PANIC! Winds of the storm won't last long
They'll make your roots tough, to grow deep and long
So little gum, bend to the storm and grow strong

3. Little Gum growing up with roots way down deep
OH NO, Worms in my roots, making me creep
A horrible feeling disturbing my sleep
Wriggling worms squirming all in a heap

4. Kooka laughing with good news bearing
DON'T PANIC! Worms work at your soil airing
Underground worms are so dirty but daring
Helping you grow, being friendly and caring

5. Gum tree is growing tall,
so more creatures come calling
OH NO! Strange creatures climbing and clawing
Cicadas drumming, hundreds of centipedes crawling
Cockroaches, scorpions up my trunk, stalking!

6. Kooka friend laughing, so happy and keen
DON'T PANIC! Scorpions and centipedes clean
Cockroaches eat litter leaves like a machine
Cicadas sing cheerily to keep you serene!

7. Gum getting used to all the ground creatures, but,
OH NO! Invaded! Huge koalas,
sugar gliders and possums
Munching and crunching in branches! Those thieves!
All night long they're eating my leaves

8. Kooka laughing, dancing and prancing
DON'T PANIC! They sleep all day, those night creatures
Won't eat much, leaves re-grow on your branches
Accept all creatures, just take your chances

9. River-red Gum tree all of a-fluster
OH NO NO! Thousands of beetles, bug insects all cluster
Stick insects, moths flapping all in a-muster
Invading, buzzing and oh what a buster!

10. Old Kooka pocking her head out of a hole
DON'T PANIC! Others will keep all control
Leaf-tailed gecko works under bark whole
Loves eating insects, to take quite a toll!

11. Poor old grandpa Gum, having more frights
OH NO! Nightmare stuff! Millions of termites!
Billions and trillions each taking their bites
They'll eat me all up, those nasty white mites

12. Listen to wise Aunty Kooka sitting down for a rest
DON'T PANIC! Holes they're all making a nest
Re-making trunk, as a place for a guest
Hollows for homes so the birds will be blessed

13. Birds of all colours are coming, flying along
OH NO! Squarks, noise and bustle seems wrong
Cockatoo, lorakeet, do they belong?
Playing and flying, they sing in a throng

14. Aunt Kooka is laughing, Gum smiling with a sigh
DON'T PANIC! We're just fun, birds up on high
We join the party, spread seeds far and wide
Keep you all growing, surviving with pride

15. Old Grumpy Gum finally laughing out loud
Oh Yes, I've survived the whole great big crowd!
Now I can welcome all creatures, they're allowed!
Party for all! So let's shout and be proud!

Drawing by Alice Jefferies, 2012
for our children's picture book with the same words.

Song of hope

Song by Dr Julie Morsillo, 2010

An Hazari refugee, at the Asylum Seeker Resource Centre, where I was the Counselling Co-ordinator, challenged me to write this song, after he read my children's book on *Finding a home*, that he felt was written for refugees trying to find a new safe home.

Once upon a time
a little bird
Felt safe and snug and warm
In her comfy nest
with her Mum and Dad
To give her all their care.

Then the storm clouds came
She was tossed about
Her world turned upside down
Her parents flew
away from her
And she was left alone.

Hold on to your hope
Little bird hold on
Hold on to your dignity
Look beyond the storms
Reach beyond the fears
Fly onto your place of hope

So the little bird knew
that it was time
to fly away from fears
In search of a
brave new world
Of peace and sanctuary

After flying for
a long long time
She found her place of rest
Where all was calm
and she felt care
A place to call her home

Hold on to your hope
Little bird hold on
Hold on to your dignity
Look beyond the storms
Reach beyond the fears
Fly onto your place of hope

Sacred Kingfisher & chick drawing by Alice Jefferies
in Finding a home, Dr Julie Morsillo, children's book.

TUNE

Inspired by a Finnish folk song, On Suuri,
that I sung when part of the
Brunswick Women's Choir
late 90s to early 2000s.

On suuri sun rantas autis - Finnish folk song
arr. Matti Hyökki, Gondwana Voices 2010
www.youtube.com/watch?v=JvezeDomChk

Tough tattooed girl
Poem by Dr Julie Morsillo, 2021

Poem inspired by a case study in a narrative therapy book:
Trauma: Narrative responses to traumatic experiences,
Edited by Dr David Denborough (2006), Dulwich Centre.

She was in trouble again
Life had been hard
She was angry and bitter
Living on the streets
Pick up by the cops again
Told to go to counselling
or back into Juvenile Justice, Prison.

She did not want to be there
Always the workers saw her as the problem
The wild child with anger issues
Lashing out at others
Hurting others, hurting herself.

She did not want to be belittled again
Asked why she was in trouble, again
She was ready to bolt
To take offence and bolt.
But the counsellor could see the fear
See the pain and distress.

The counsellor gently asked:
What are your hopes and dreams?
What do you want from life?
If you could have anything,
what would it be?

The tough tattooed girl
Burst into tears.
No-one has ever asked her that before
They always wanted to know
why she stuffed up, again
But now someone asking for her dreams.

Well my dream is to be called 'My princess.'
Now it was the counsellor's
turn to be surprised.
This butch girl, wanting to be a princess?
Not what she was expecting.

The girl explained
That is what my Dad would call me
Before my world fell apart.
The counsellor had helped her
To light a candle in the darkness of her life
To remember the ray of light
To cling to, to build upon,
To find a way forward.
To be a princess, again.

Dr David Denborough book
Denborough, D. (2006) *Trauma: Narrative responses to traumatic experiences*.
Dulwich Centre Publications

Dr David Denborough presentation
Exchanging stories, skills and songs:
The possibilities of narrative practice
www.youtube.com/watch?v=hU1-DL8jRHY

Distraught father
Poem by Dr Julie Morsillo, 2021

A distraught father
could not come to terms
with his son's life choices.
He was appalled
His son had gender dysphoria
Was taking steps to change into a girl
to become a daughter.
All the father's dreams shattered.
He hoped his son would grow into a man
Whom he could be proud of.

He rang a telephone counselling
helpline a few times.
The counsellor sought my support.
I suggested to acknowledge his pain
Gently ask him to perhaps
Consider that his child is
Still the same precious child
He had cradled and supported as a babe
Deep down the child was the same.
Now the child just wanted to change clothes
from the dull boring boyish clothes
to bright colourful clothes
to shine in a different more creative way in the world.

Still the same treasured child with his DNA
just a more creative appearance
The father was given permission
to consider a new perspective
to light a candle into his darkness
to find a pathway forward.
To embrace his child again.
The father did just that.
Love trumped fear.

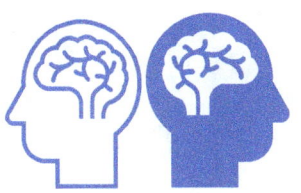

Poem inspiration
from supervision for a Master of Community Counselling
student at Eastern College Australia (2021)

Sunny Millar Ted Talk
Life with gender dysphoria (2018)
www.youtube.com/watch?v=M9YICZZeJNs

Royal Children's Hospital Website
Gender Service: trans & gender diverse
www.rch.org.au/adolescent-medicine/gender-service/

The water of life
Chester Cathedral, UK
Sculpture by Dr Stephen Smalley, 1994

This sculpture is based on a bible story of Jesus asking a Samaritan woman for a drink of water at a well. At the time, it was unheard of, for a Jewish man to speak to a Gentile woman. This is an empowering moment for a woman rejected by her community.

Dr Stephen Smalley – Broadbent studio
https://broadbent.studio/water-of-life

Sculpture intentions by Dr Stephen Smalley

*"My intentions with the piece
were to show an intensity of relationship,
in such, at that very moment,
there was no one else existing in the world.*

*In its sculptural form,
I felt Christ needed to be set
below this remarkable woman,
while at the same time revealing
how her life was springing out from his.
I also wanted to show some ambiguity
as to who was giving the water,
and importantly for the water
to be overflowing.*

*It was the tenderness of Christ
that touched me personally,
her shame was to be taken away
and not paraded across her community,
with whom she became wonderfully reconciled."*

The woman found her redemptive story,
her own song to sing.

1.7 Narrative therapy for hopeful life stories

Narrative therapy - strength-based approach
Concept by Michael White & David Epston

Narrative therapy is a s strength-based approach, developed by *Michael White* and *David Epston*, colleagues from Adelaide, Australia, and New Zealand. Narrative therapy, can help us to retell our stories of despair and shame, to find our meaningful redemptive stories.

Narrative therapy separates the person from the problem, and asks questions like:

– How has anxiety or depression affected your life?

– How might you respond differently, remembering unique times when the problem was lessened?

– What supports do you have (or supports that could used)?

– How might you use those supports and your own skills more effectively?

This can strengthen the positive hopeful stories, remembering the good times when some joy and some support were experienced.

Michael White books
White, M. (1995). *Re-authoring lives: Interviews & essays*. Adelaide, SA: Dulwich Centre Publications.

White, M. (2007). *Maps of narrative practice*. W.W. Norton.

Michael White & David Epston book
White, M., & Epston, D. (1990). *Narrative means to therapeutic ends*. W. W. Norton.

Narrative therapy aim
To separate the individual from the issue, and externalise problems instead of internalising them.

Narrative therapy concepts
– Respectful of client
– Non-blaming
– Client is expert of own life

Narrative therapy techniques
– Telling one's story (narrative)
– Externalising problem technique
– Deconstruction technique
– Unique outcomes technique
– Existentialism

Narrative therapy metaphors
Narrative therapy metaphors for hopeful life stories, have been developed to work with various groups in a variety of cultural and aged-based settings. These can also be adapted to use in individual counselling work. (See over page for more)

Narrative therapy principles & techniques
https://positivepsychology.com/narrative-therapy/

Michael White talk
Trauma & Narrative Therapy (2007)
https://vimeo.com/34671797

David Epston talk
How do we come to know whose who seek our help? (2021)
www.youtube.com/watch?v=oNUxWBRjb7A

Narrative therapy metaphors
for positive life stories

Tree of Life metaphor
Concept by Dr David Denborough
and narrative therapist communities

Tree of Life is a narrative therapy metaphor, first developed to help orphans after genocide find a redemptive story. This metaphor can be useful for anyone or any group of people.

*__Roots__ of the tree represents the positive aspects of the **past**, the family traditions, the cultural festivals, the rituals in everyday life, the special times. All to help build the positive hopeful stories in life.

*__Ground__ with the daily activities of life that bring some satisfaction.

*__Trunk__ to explore our own **personal skills** and what they enjoyed doing, from cooking to music and art, and strengthen the sense of identity, that you do have something to offer, to bring joy within, and maybe to others too.

*__Branches__ to represent the **hopes and dreams** in our lives, to remember where there is life there is hope.

*__Leaves__ are the supports in our lives, whose who have given of themselves to you, family and friends and community groups.

*__Fruit or seeds,__ the gifts you have given others.

NOTE:
The *Storms of life* can be explored, after strengthening identity with the TREE of LIFE first. The STORMS of LIFE is the concept of tackling the problems of life, but after strengthening own identity to help deal with the problems. (So using the strengths of the person, to help with any weakness or problems).

David Denborough book on
Narrative Therapy with Tree of Life
(highly recommended – easy to read - inexpensive)
Denborough, D. (2014). *Retelling the stories of our lives: Everyday narrative therapy to draw inspiration and transform experience.* W.W. Norton.

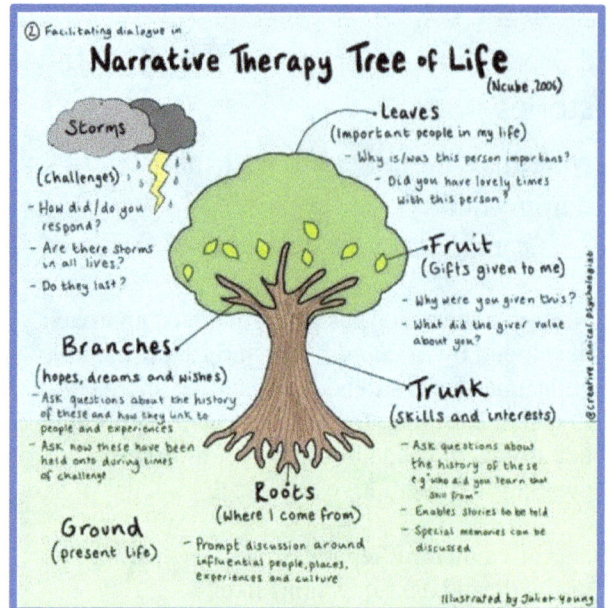

Drawing by Juliet Young
Creative Clinical Psychologist
www.julietyoung.co.uk

NOTE:
This narrative therapy metaphor, the Tree of Life, was first developed with orphaned children from communities suffering with HIV-AIDS in South Africa, and with children suffering from genocide in Rwanda. At first the children were told that if their leaves of support included those who had died, like their parents and grandparents, then the leaves could be drawn as fallen to the ground. However, the children began to cry, remembering their terrible loss of no longer having their parents or grandparents in their daily lives. So, the narrative therapists came up with a different idea. The leaves could all stay in the trees, because those leaves of support, even if they were physically no longer with us, emotionally, they were still close to us in our hearts, and in our DNA, and in the legacy that they have left us. So they are still living leaves in our lives that can still influence us, and we can still learn and respond as they have taught us.

Tree of Life metaphor projects
Dulwich Centre. (2019) Tree of Life Projects.
https://dulwichcentre.com.au/the-tree-of-life/

Tree of Life presentation
Using the Tree of Life tool to talk about stories of hope and resilience by Anees Hakim (2020)
www.youtube.com/watch?v=rkPcXu_4sds

Worksheet I – Tree of Life metaphor

Draw an outline of a tree. Imagine yourself as this tree. Write descriptions in and around your tree, related to the different aspects of the tree of life:

ROOTS – *family traditions, festivals, holidays*

GROUND – *daily life activities of satisfaction*

TRUNK – *personal skills, interests, fun activities*

BRANCHES – *values, hopes & dreams*

LEAVES – *supports in past & present*

SEEDS – *gifts or support given to others*

Drawing by Alice Jefferies, 2012

Prompts to begin

This is a narrative therapy metaphor, developed to help bring back some positive life-giving narratives, especially after some tough times, when life is filled with sadness and distress. So, for the purpose of this exercise, this is a time to think only of the positive and hopeful times in life. This recalling and re-membering of meaningful times, can help to survive the losses, and move forward in life again, to develop our own song to soar.

NOTE: When I was training counsellors with this metaphor, in Cambodia and in the Prague Synagogue (2019), the counsellors expressed their appreciation to help to remember the good and positive aspects about their culture and families (after genocide), their own skills and supports, to strengthen their hopeful identity narrative, so help to sing a song to soar in life.

Tree of Life metaphor projects
Dulwich Centre. (2019) Tree of Life Projects. See website:
https://dulwichcentre.com.au/the-tree-of-life/

Tree of Life presentation
Tree of Life: Working with vulnerable children (2022)
www.youtube.com/watch?v=L9gVKMxjUvU

Other narrative therapy metaphors

Team of life metaphor
Concept by Viviane Oliveira, 2009

Team of Life metaphor was developed with refugee young men who loved playing soccer, but reluctant to talk about their personal lives. The young men were able to open up using the team metaphor to explore who was on their team of life.

Who is on your team, wing person, coach, caterer, and first-aid person?

1. Developing team sheet
- Re-membering who is on your team of life (i.e. choosing the members of your team)
- Who are your faithful team member friends?
- Who is your coach, caterer, first-aid officer?
- Who will be relegated to the side-lines?

2. Celebrating goals
- Re-membering goals achieved already (to strengthen identity)

3. Tackling problems
- Exchange knowledge of how to tackle problems

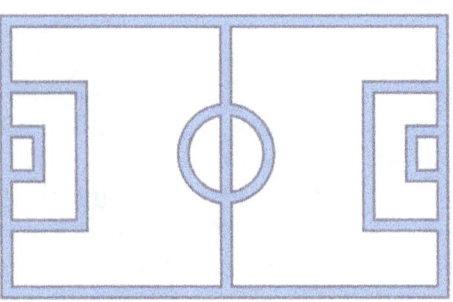

Team of Life article
Oliveira, V. (2009). Team Garra: using the Team of Life to facilitate conversations with Brazilians living in Sydney. *International Journal of Narrative Therapy and Community Work*, 4, pp. 52–61.

Team of Life projects
Narrative Therapy at Dulwich Centre, Adelaide
https://dulwichcentre.com.au/team-of-life/

Team of Life presentation
Team of Life: A collective narrative methodology offering young people a sporting chance
By Dr David Denborough (2024)
www.youtube.com/watch?v=K5u5SdsNdkY

Worksheet J – Team of Life metaphor

Imagine all the people that support you in life, as part of your team of life.

What roles do your supports play? For example, this could be the following:

COACH – provide regular encouragement

TEAM members – faithful friends

CATERER – provides food or coffees at times

FIRST-AID – sympathy with shoulder to cry on

SIDE-LINED – rarely supportive

Prompts
See more on previous page

Background
Young men can be reluctant to talk about themselves and their feelings, or to seek help in times of trouble. However, some can talk about their favourite sport or favourite activity with friends. So this narrative therapy metaphor was developed especially for young refugee men who lived and breathed soccer.

NOTE: However, in the training of counsellors in Melbourne, I had an older woman who loved this metaphor, but adapted it to her non–sporting life. So, instead of coaches and team players, she had the caterer and the first-aid person (her daughter and friends). She also liked the idea of relegating unsupportive family members to the side-lines. Thus, not being rejected totally, but kept at a distance to protect herself, until they showed themselves worthy of being a player on her team.

List your team of life players and roles

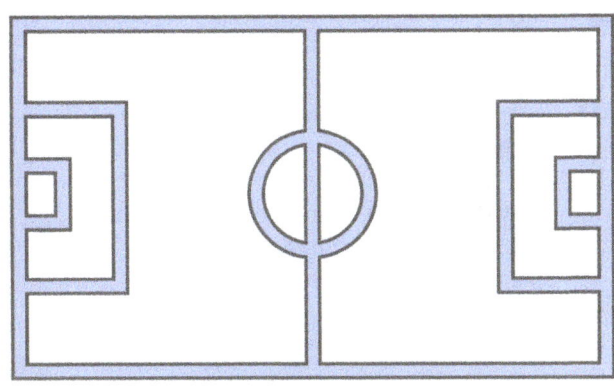

Team of Life projects
Narrative Therapy at Dulwich Centre, Adelaide website:
https://dulwichcentre.com.au/team-of-life/

Team of Life presentation
Team of Life: Offering young people a sporting chance (2024)
www.youtube.com/watch?v=K5u5SdsNdkY

See more creative ideas at end of this section 1.9 & 1.10
Creative counselling with children
Creative work with youth

Kite of life metaphor
Concept by Dr David Denborough, 2010

The kite has special meaning in some cultures, being used in festivals and play.

A kite can represent the feeling of freedom and flying high in life, to soar in life.

The Kite of Life metaphor was developed to help with **intergenerational conflict,** of children or youth, in conflict with parents or grandparents, over their differences (like traditional verses modern ways of thinking and behaving). This metaphor was developed to find the common ground, in some **common cultural values, hopes and dreams,** like at festival or fun times together.

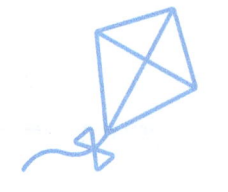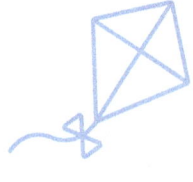

The concept of a kite flying free (or perhaps some kind of bird, like a kite, similar to a hawk) can be discussed. Then questions on common values like:

- How do we help others who are in despair?
- How do we calm them?
- How do we help them in their relationships?
- How can we help them see their common values?
- How do we help them to re-member their redemptive story of hope?

Kite of Life booklet
Denborough, D. (2010). *Kite of life: From intergenerational conflict to intergenerational alliance.* Dulwich Centre Foundation.

Kite of Life presentation
Kite of Life: Intergenerational conflict to alliance (2011)
https://vimeo.com/18946312

Worksheet K – Kite of Life metaphor

Think of a difficult relationship, such as intergenerational conflict.
What common hopes and dreams do you have across the generations?
Write these in the kite. For example, this could include concept like:

VALUES of CARING – times when kind to each other

BELIEF in FAMILY – caring for family members

RELIGIOUS or SPIRITUAL beliefs in common

SIMILAR DREAMS – peaceful co-existence

HOPES in common – travel and enjoying life

Prompts
See more prompt questions on previous page

Kites can represent the freedom and fun of flying high, of life when you can soar.

Talk about what kites represent for the client, family or group. In some cultures they have kite festivals as special fun events for everyone.

Talk about fun times, special times, happier times with family, sharing common hopes and dreams. To remember times when you sang a song to soar in life.

A sample song that expresses the freedom of kites:
Let's go fly a kite by Richard & Robert Sheeman
Song for Mary Poppins Disney Movie, 1964.
Provided to YouTube by Universal Music Group, 2020.
https://www.youtube.com/watch?v=6KO---qgvDI

Draw a kite

Write hopes and dreams in the kite

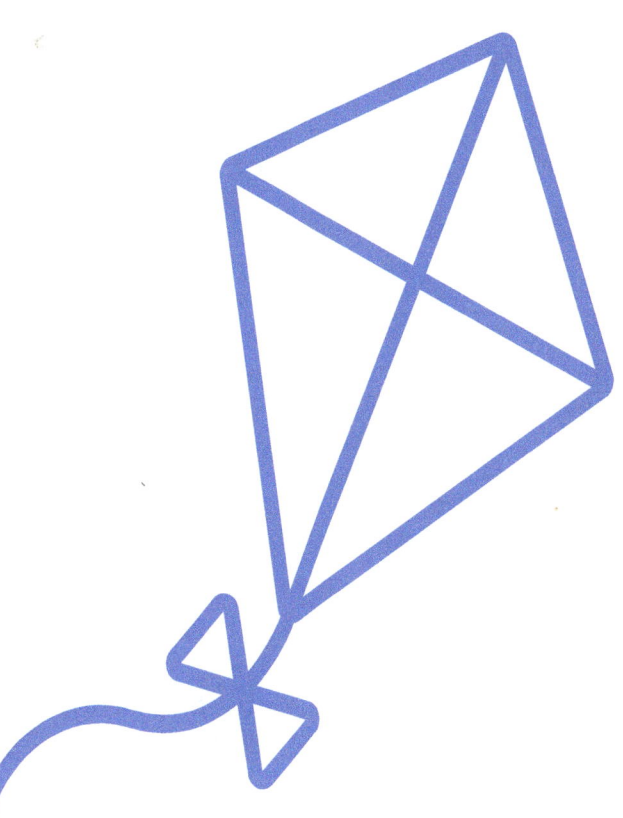

Kite of Life workshops
https://dulwichcentre.com.au/intergenerational-conflict/the-kite-of-life-workshop/

Crossing the River metaphor
Concept by Therese Hegarty, Greg Smith, & Mark Hammersley

The narrative therapy, Crossing the River metaphor, was developed for those wanting to give up addictions. It can also be used with those wanting to make lifestyle changes.

Firstly, what are the goals to get to the other side of the river? Then, consider what has to be given up, before crossing the river. Lastly, what specific steps need to be taken to cross the river, in order to get to the other side?

Consider:

1. What **goals** do you have in life?

2. What **changes** might you make in your life to cross the river, or to change direction in your life?

3. What might you have to **give up** in order to make a significant change in life (including any friends)?

4. What might you **bring back** into your life?

5. Re-calling **what brings joy in life** - music, art, dance, laughter, time with friends, creativity, or whatever.

Crossing a river in Abel Tasman National Park, NZ.

Crossing the River article
Hegarty, T., Smith, G., & Hammersley, M (2010). Crossing the river: A metaphor for separation, liminality and reincorporation, *International Journal of Narrative and Community Work, No 2, 2010, Dulwich Centre.*

Worksheet L – Crossing the River metaphor

Think of a lifestyle change you might like to make in your life. This could be:

_____

GIVING UP an addiction

CHANGING job or workplace or studies

CHANGING a relationship

CHANGING your diet

CHANGING your regular exercise

_____

DRAW a river
1. Write on other side:
What might you gain and bring back in life (friends, fun, joy)?

2, Write on side where you are:
What you need to give up or change? Any change in supports?

3. Write in river *(stepping stones or raft)*: What steps are needed to cross the river

What needs to be given up?

What else will be lost?

What will be gained?

What supports to help?

What steps are needed to get across the river?

Photo of Maribyrnong River, Melbourne

Prompt to begin
When trying to give up an addiction or making a change in life-style, we often think about the gains we could make by changing. But we also need to consider what we have to give up, which could include long-held habits and friends that we enjoyed at some stage. So the extra losses need to be considered and worked through, to realise the extent of the change and be prepared. Then to be reminded of the gains and the steps needed to get there, to help develop your own song to soar.

Crossing the River article
Hegarty, T., Smith, G., & Hammersley, M (2010). Crossing the river: A metaphor for separation, liminality and reincorporation, *International Journal of Narrative and Community Work, No 2, 2010, Dulwich Centre.*

Life Certificate metaphor

Concept by Mohamed Fareez, 2015.

The Life Certificate narrative therapy metaphor, was developed to help those suffering from terrible grief and loss.

So with a death certificate we record the finality of a person's life, with details of their birth, and how they died.

Whereas, with a Life Certificate, we can **honour the legacy** that they have left us, and remember what they have taught us, and the joy that they brought to our lives. We can still hold these memories in our heart and mind.

This legacy is ongoing. So a Life Certificate can be made, to celebrate that our loved one is still in our memories and our heart. Also, if family, they are in our very DNA. We may not be here without them.

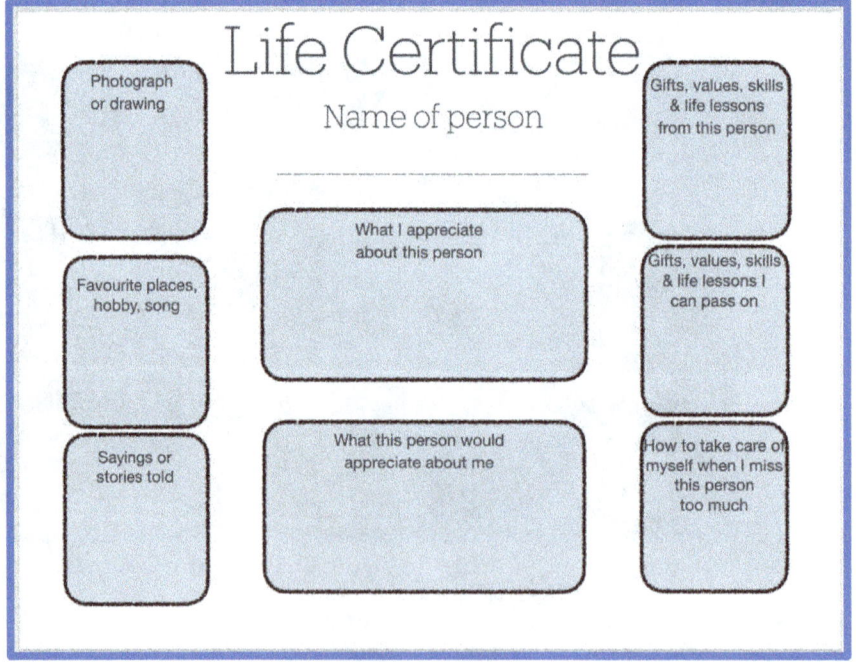

Life Certificate article
Fareez, M. (2015). The 'Life Certificate': A tool for grief work in Singapore. The International Journal of Narrative Therapy and Community Work. Vol 2.

Life Certificate presentation
Narrative therapy: Life Certificate for grief & loss (2018)
www.youtube.com/watch?v=HImiFzdRfCY

Worksheet M – Life Certificate metaphor

Name someone close to you who is gone.

Describe them and what they taught you?

Complete the Life Certificate

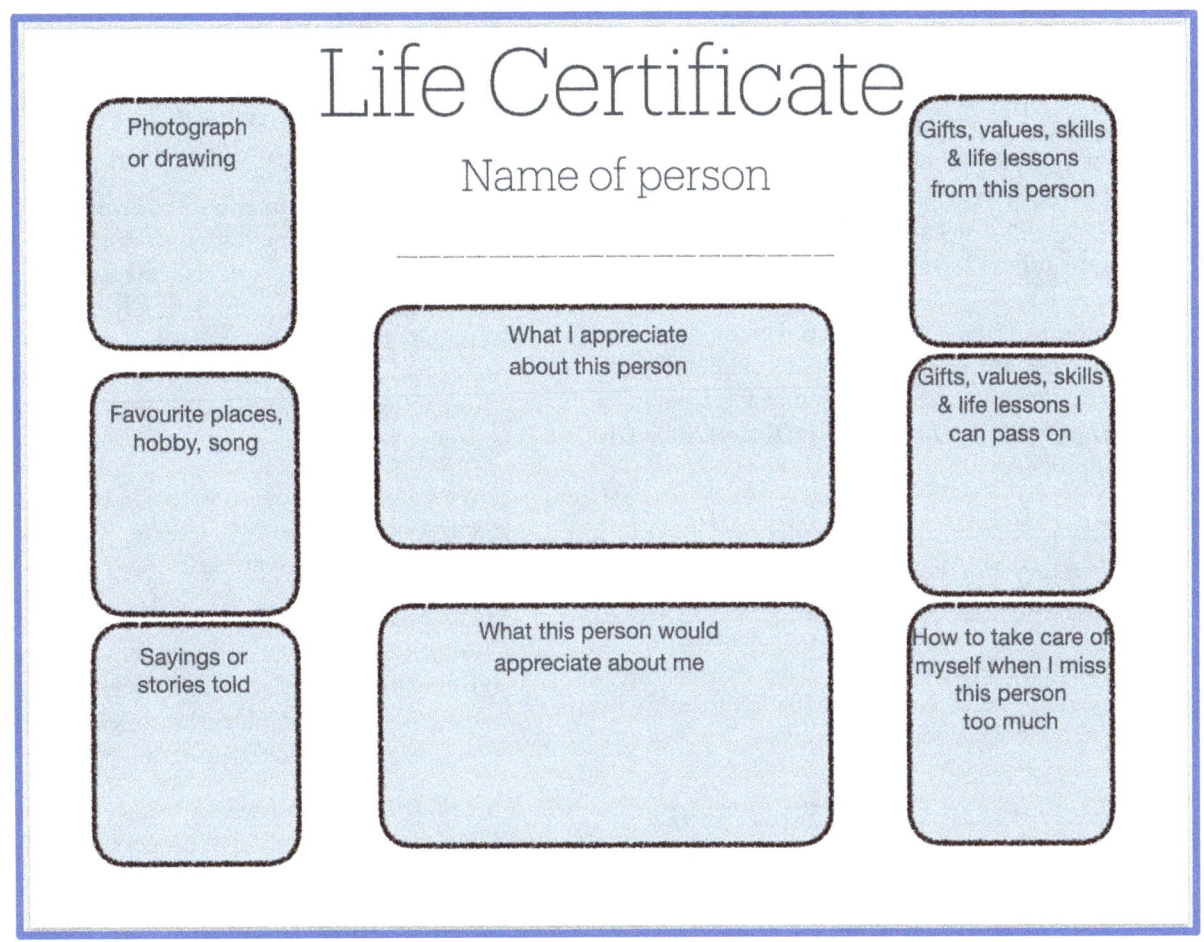

Prompts
It can be very hard to say goodbye to someone we love. But, we can still carry them in our hearts and in our memories, being thankful for what they have taught us, and the legacy that they have left us.

'Say hello again: When we have lost someone we love' article
Michael White, co-founder of narrative therapy (2004)
https://dulwichcentre.com.au/wp-content/uploads/2020/01/Saying_hello_again_when_we_have_lost_someone_we_love.pdf?fbclid=IwAR3Mx6ufbwwtpkl1b8xg3qC5nOzNVva_QqqH5uk-_HnWDu6JBb0hn0mvaR8

Life Certificate article
Fareez, M. (2015). The 'Life Certificate': A tool for grief work in Singapore. The International Journal of Narrative Therapy and Community Work. Vol 2.

Life Certificate presentation
Narrative therapy: Life Certificate for grief & loss (2018)
www.youtube.com/watch?v=HImiFzdRfCY

1.8 Self-compassion and Compassion focused therapy

Self-compassion
Concept by Prof Kirstin Neff

Taking care of ourselves is most important. We need self-care that is compassionate towards ourselves. Care for our social and emotional wellbeing, our physical wellbeing, our mental wellbeing, and our relational and social wellbeing. We often **neglect ourselves**, and think negatively of ourselves, that, in turn, can then adversely affect our relationships with others. If we neglect ourselves to the point of becoming unwell or depressed, or experiencing **compassion fatigue**, then we cannot sustainably continue in our quest to **care for others** or help others or develop respectful relationships We need to develop our meaningful stories, where we remember the positive hopeful stories from our younger days, and strengthen those stories that become our redemptive stories from our past that informs who we are today.

Self-compassion concept has been explored by *Prof Kirsten Neff,* as she describes the need, to **feel positive about ourselves**, **and not listening to negative voices, or being a perfectionist**, constantly berating ourselves. This only leaves us in a negative state, with not much left to enjoy life, or to give compassion to others.

SELF-COMPASSION is:
Mindfulness
Self-kindness
Connectedness

Prof Kristin Neff & Prof Christopher Germer
Workbook & website
Neff, K. D. & Germer, C. K (2018). *The mindful self-compassion workbook: A program proven way to accept yourself, find your inner strength and thrive.* Guilford Press.
https://self-compassion.org/self-compassion-practices/#self-compassion-exercises

Prof Christopher Germer presentation
Mindful self-compassion (2020)
www.youtube.com/watch?v=igOBO1RfUtc

Self-compassion exercises
Exercises by Prof Kristin Neff & Prof Christopher Germer

1 How would you treat a friend
How might you responded to yourself in the same way you respond to a close friend when they are suffering?

2 Self-compassion break
Remember a time when feeling stressed. This is just a moment of suffering, a part of life. Now with hand on heart feeling the warmth, thinking: May I be kind to myself and accept myself.

3 Exploring self-compassion through writing
Everybody has something they don't like about themselves, causing some shame and feeling not "good enough." Now think of a friend or religious person who is perfectly accepting and values you. Write a letter to yourself about this, from a place of acceptance and compassion.

4 Supportive touch
Give yourself a supportive touch, to active your parasympathetic nervous system, to help you feel calm, cared for and safe.

5 Changing your critical self-talk
Acknowledging your self-critical voice and reframe this in a more friendly way, to eventually form the blueprint for changing how you relate to yourself long-term.

6 Self-compassion journal
Keeping a daily journal to process difficult events of your day, through a lens of self-compassion, enhancing both mental and physical well-being. This can help make self-kindness, common humanity, and mindfulness part of your daily life.

7 Identifying what we really want
Remember that to motivate yourself, love is more powerful than fear. Reframe your inner dialogue, for more positive responses, to be more encouraging and supportive.

8 Taking care of the caregiver
Give yourself time to meet your own needs, keeping your heart open and help you care for and nurture yourself. This will help you to have more caring and nurturing towards others.#

Worksheet N – Self-Compassion

How would your closest friend describe you? Your traits, values and skills. What have you given to others in life? This could be values like:

_____

KINDNESS – considerate, caring, empathetic

HELPFUL – there when needed

BRING JOY – make others laugh

SHARE time over coffee

GIVING – generous

_____

Prompts
When we feel discouraged about relationships or life, we can neglect to care for ourselves and forget to appreciate what we can do and forget what we have given to others.

So imagine what a close friend might say about you and what you have given to them or given to others
List these skills and gifts you have given over the years

Now think of what you can do to care for yourself
Something that brings joy or a smile
Something that relaxes, or inspires you
Take time to do this on a regular basis, so no burnout.

What brings you JOY, to be inspired, have fun or relax? Perhaps:

_____

MUSIC – listen, play, accompany

ART – create artwork, photogrphy

MOVEMENT – team sport, dancing, exercise

WALKING, running or riding

READING or MOVIES – fiction, non-fiction, docos

_____

Prof Kristin Neff & Christopher Germer workbook
Neff, K. D. & Germer, C. K (2018). *The mindful self-compassion workbook: A program proven way to accept yourself, find your inner strength and thrive.* Guilford Press.

Prof Kristin Neff presentation
Mindfulness & Self-compassion (2013)
www.youtube.com/watch?v=qqQHhF4CaKQ

53

Compassion Focused Therapy
Concept by Dr Paul Gilbert OBE, 2018.

Compassion focused therapy (CFT) developed by *Dr Paul Gilbert*, is about building self-compassion for oneself, and in turn have more compassion towards others, for respectful relationships and an improved sense of wellbeing. We need to feel valued within ourselves, to order to add value to our relationships and to the community, for a value-based community redemptive story.

(cp. *Mattering by Prof Isaac Prilleltensky, 2014*)

Our lives are constantly lived in relationship with others, so we need to relate well to those around us. We need to show compassion, by seeking ways to be caring and nurturing, and responding in ways that are co-operative and sharing, rather than competitive.

Dr Paul Gilbert book
Gilbert, P. (2018). Introducing compassion focused therapy. Cambridge Core. Cambridge University Press

Dr Paul Gilbert presentation
How mindfulness fosters compassion (2013)
www.youtube.com/watch?v=pz9Fr_v9Okw

Dr Paul Gilbert & colleagues' website
Compassionate Mind Foundation, UK (2006-2024)
https://www.compassionatemind.co.uk

Compassionate imagery
Dr Paul Gilbert has developed forms of compassionate imagery to help in developing more compassion for oneself, and in turn, more compassion for others, for mutual benefits.

Compassion attention
*Remembering when you have shown courage, been kind to others, or previous coping strategies in difficult situations

*Appreciate and savour the experience of positive attributes

*Develop gratitude for good things in life - taste of food, colours of sky, nature, music

Compassion reasoning
*Use CBT & DBT to question thinking and come to better reasoning and more compassion towards self,
to lift shame and guilt

Compassion behaviour
*Spirit of compassion towards self-warmth, compassion and gentleness towards self
(like a parent encouraging a child)

*Learning to deal with threats, by being more assertive (not submissive)

*Learn to be brave and courageous (not fearful) of facing new situations or enjoying nice things – being process focused (rather than task)

Compassion imagery
*Exercises to generate compassionate feeling towards self

*Explore ideal compassionate self

*Can you imagine yourself as an animal or tree or mountain? What kind?

Worksheet O – Compassion Focused Therapy

Compassionate attention, such as:

_____

Time when KIND to others

Time when showed COURAGE

Time when HELPFUL to others

Time when you GAVE generously

Compassionate behaviours, such as:

_____

Think of ways to be GENEROUS towards self

Think of times when showed COURAGE

ENCOURAGE yourself like you would a child

Remember times when you HELPED others

Compassionate reasoning, such as:

_____

Time when felt SHAME but others to blame

Time when felt GUILTY but did your best

Time when told not GOOD enough but did try

Time when overcame a THREAT

Compassionate imagery, such as:

_____

Think of times at your BEST

Remember when you GAVE much to others

Imagine self as an ANIMAL or tree

Imagine your IDEAL self

Prompt
We can feel shame and guilt about things done to us. But really the shame and guilt are often external, a community issue of power and threats. We can release our shame and guilt, which only hurts yourself, and instead be compassionate towards ourselves.

Dr Paul Gilbert presentation on compassion
Compassion Focused Therapy workshop (2013)
www.youtube.com/watch?v=qnHuECDlSvE

My prayer
    Song by Julie Morsillo, 1983

May my life be a prayer
Journeying towards God
Wanting only to serve all
A discipline of love
A discipline of love.

May my words be ever kind
Others to encourage
Careful not to criticise
But speak of good alone
Speak of good alone.

May my actions be always pure
Working for the common good
Striving for justice everywhere
Not hurting anyone
Not hurting anyone

May my heart be filled with love
Seeking purity of thought
Caring for all creation
With a spirit of joy
With a spirit of Joy
WITH A SPIRIT OF JOY.

> The fruit of the spirit is
> **love, joy, peace, patience, kindness, goodness, faithfulness, gentleness and self-control,**
> against such things
> there is no low.
> Galations5: 22-23

Dr Julie Morsillo interview podcast
Faith and Identity (2018)
https://ultimateyouthworker.com.au/2018/05/faith-and-identity/?_ga=2.255432960.901461188.1720142354-2054609077.1720142354

Personal loving kindness meditation

The loving-kindness meditation starts by nurturing and growing kindness toward ourselves, with self-compassion

It is one way to reflect on our own life story and focus on the beautiful and hopeful moments.

Times when strength has enabled you to overcome adversity. Times when you felt compassion, cherished and cared for by other people. Times when you witnessed beauty in nature, an artwork or a moment in someone else's life.

Steps

Begin this meditation by finding a comfortable space away from distraction and responsibility.

Acknowledge that you by setting aside this time, you are already choosing to nurture yourself.

Take three deep breaths through the mouth and feel your stomach expand. Exhale through the nose and feel the sensation of movement of your breath.

Now start to focus on feelings of peace and calm. You can imagine a beautiful place or song to cultivate the feeling of calm.

An affirmation such as "I am safe and at peace" can also be repeated.

Next, allow the feeling of peace to grow into a feelings of strength and confidence. This is a chance to focus on moments of your life where you have overcome adversity or bravely tried something new.

Any examples of times that you have shown strength.

Lastly, allow the feeling of strength to expand out into a feeling of love toward yourself. Focus on the beautiful moments of your life and the beautiful values you hold.

Acknowledge that you are flawed and simultaneously infinitely beautiful.

You are perfect in every way
by Laura Boys (student, 2021).

Let your freckles
Wrinkles
And eye crinkles
Be works of art
Touch the silvery line-work stretchmarks
The pockmarks of a teen now adult
And marvel at the body that tells a story
Hug your rounded curves or slightly frame
Your petite chest or soft round tummy
And whisper to yourself,
Like a mother to a child
You are perfect in every way.

Loving-kindness mediation
Adapted from
Mindful: Healthy mind, healthy life
www.mindful.org/this-loving-kindness-meditation-is-a-radical-act-of-love/

More on self-compassion
Prof Kristin Neff Ted Talk
Self-esteem & self-compassion (2013)
www.youtube.com/watch?v=IvtZBUSplr4

Pandemic to rock the world: From plague to recovery
Poem by Dr Julie Morsillo, 2021

A plague on your house
Like a war that is prolonged
Interned in concentration camp
Locked in detention centre
with no known end in sight
A pandemic to rock the world

Isolation to stop the spread
Limits to travel
Limits to socialising
Limits to events
Limits to family times
Limits to friendship
Limits to classrooms
No end of limits
With no end in sight

Isolation for our protection
To stop the spread of harm
So our health is preserved
So our vulnerable don't die
So our kids don't get sick
So we live to see another day

So thankful for healthcare workers
For those who develop vaccinations
For nurses and doctors caring for us
Not isolating to protect us from further harm

Grateful for all workers
Growing food for us
Distributing food and goods for us
Cleaning for us
Providing hospitality for us
Helping those in need

We are not really fighting each other
Or fighting fires and floods as often
Or even fighting a common enemy
Except the unseen enemy of a plague

Yet, we know that the plague
Will eventually run out of puff
Die down to just a whimper of a cold
Back to just the normal ills
That often can be treated

But still we need to care for each other
And care for our planet
So we can continue to live
Our grandchildren can continue to live
Live a valued and valuable life

Hopefully this pandemic will
Rock us out of our complacency
Giving us liminal time to re-evaluate
To work out what really matters
Needing to care for each other
Care for the planet

Prepare for further climate changes
Prepare for more bushfires
For more floods and plagues
Protect the planet and animals
Keep the trees alive
As they keep us alive

Be rocked from our complacency
Start a revolution of kindness
A kindness pandemic
To save the world
To save our souls
To save our children
Our future #

UNPRECEDENTED TIMES CALL FOR UNPRECEDENTED KINDNESS

Inspired by
Dr Catherine Barrett webpage & Facebook
The Kindness Pandemic (2020)
www.thekindnesspandemic.org
Dr Catherine Barrett interview
The Kindness Pandemic (2020)
www.youtube.com/watch?v=WVPaQ_0P9XM

Dr Hugh Mackay interview
The joy of discovering who we really are (2020)
www.youtube.com/watch?v=nntiR-H-PC0
Dr Hugh Mackay book
Mackay, H. (2021). The kindness revolution: How we can restore hope, rebuild trust and inspire optimism. Allen & Unwin.

1.9 Finding personal meaning with children

Creative ideas for working with children

1. Play with cards
St Luke's Innovative Resources, Bendigo - strength-based card sets – for example:

a. Teddy Bears cards with each card having a different emotion portrayed by the teddy bear - children can choose any few that they like and tell stories about the bears;

b. Anxiety cards - each card has a positive strategy to overcome anxiety & plan alternate responses.

Many other sets of cards that open up stories with the children.
See more in St Luke's Innovative Resources website.

2. Puppets
Hand puppets or finger puppets, where the child chooses a puppet and talks through the puppet. Puppets could be: animals, birds, muppets, football team mascots, or heroes. Talking through the puppets is not as confronting as being questioned directly, like teachers and parents do.

3. Stones
Any river stones or bag of stones with different expressions from St Luke's Innovative Resources

4. Art Work
Drawing pictures about their feelings and issues to talk through, notice the colours used, bright or dark, and subject matter if bright or dark.

5. Family of wooden figures
(or wooden clothes pegs)

Can buy in Kmart or cheap craft or reject shop Child can nominate a family member for each figure and arrange them in relation to figure of self. You could ask:
- Which is the most important?
- Who is close to whom?
- Who has conflict?
- Who gives support?

6. Sand Play or table top
with figurines

Wooden, plastic or metal figures, figurines or pegs to represent family members or heroes or favourite activities.

Child can choose any figures and arrange the figures as they like, to tell a story or show a relationship. Ask child to talk about the figures and their importance or if a trusting or conflicting relationship.

7. Treasure box
Provide a small wooden or cardboard box with lid. Child can choose how to decorate the box. Could offer stickers to decorate the outside of the treasure box or colour pens with favourite colours or patterns.

Then talk about possible treasures or symbols of treasures that could go inside the box.

Different possibilities for the treasure box:
- Small drawings of family or heroes or favourite activities
- Figure puppets or small figures to represent favourite people or heroes
- Photos or drawings of favourite people and favourite places and favourite activities or movies
- Small shells or stones representing something special.

This treasure box (and other creative activities) can help the child feel treasured, and strengthen their sense of identity, to help them start to build up a song to sing and to soar in life
.

1.10 Finding personal meaning work with youth

Creative ideas for working with youth

1. Reflexion Cards
St Luke's Innovative Resources, Bendigo & online

Youth can choose cards that they related to at the moment - eg. alone, scared, angry - in one pile
Youth can choose cards that they want to be
- eg. creative, confident, fun, courageous, brave – in another pile. (Discard other cards)

This starts conversations to work through their worries, and strengthen their hopes and dreams. Youth like the outward focus on the cards, rather than be directly questioned personally.

2. Gym or park
Consider counselling in a school gym or parkland, where you do movement or walking together, with the young person, so they can feel like they are doing something, and talking is secondary.

3. Movies & video games heroes
Ask about favourite movies or games, and talk about the heroes, and what they offer, and then talk about what the young person might do to emulate the hero somehow.

4. Music to inspire or calm
Ask about favourite music that is inspiring or calming. Listen to the song or music piece together, if possible, and talk about why it is so inspirational or calming.
Ask about when first heard this music, and if that is emotive for them. Suggest they listen to this music when feeling sad or anxious, to give them courage again.
[See also D. Worksheet Inspiring Music]

NOTE: **Mentor programs** can be very beneficial for youth
Raise - Youth Mentoring program
https://www.raise.org.au
Stars Foundation – Mentoring Indigenous young women
www.downergroup.com/Supporting%20Indigenous%20young%20girls%20to%20succeed

5. Team of Life
Narrative Therapy metaphor, Dulwich Centre Adelaide Talk about favourite sport, and how to think about that in relation to life:
Who is on your team?
Who is our coach?
Your does first aid or caterer?
Who is on the side bench with limited time & space in life?
[See Team of Life & Worksheet D. Team of Life]

6. Acting out bullying
Remember that bullies have often been bullied themselves at home or at school., so it's a community issue. An individual or group activity:
*Talk about responses that do not help, then responses that are helpful.
*Act out unhelpful responses, then alternate responses that might be helpful
Concept from community theatre or community sports from Theatre of the Oppressed by Brazilian Augusto Boal #

Augusto Boal book online
Boal, A. (2002).Games for actors and non-actors. Routledge.
www.deepfun.com/wp-content/uploads/2010/06/Games-for-actors-and-non-actors...Augusto-Boal.pdf

7. Community service
Youth who spend time helping others, tend to have a better sense of wellbeing and stronger sense of identity for resilience in life.
Community service examples:
- Cooking together for a community event, like a church lunch
- Visiting an aged care home and talking with elderly about their lives when they were young
- Practical help to grandparents or neighbour with shopping, gardening, mowing, housework
- Babysitting for friends, family or neighbours

Giving to others can help to build a sense of identity and sense of community connectedness for their own song to sing and soar in life.

Resilience Project:
Gratitude, Empathy & Mindfulness (GEM)
by Hugh van Cuylenburg (2022)
https://theresilienceproject.com.au/media-posts/resilience-and-happiness-depend-on-gratitude-empathy-and-mindfulness/

Part 2 – **O**ther respectful relationships beside us

2.1 Life in relationship with others

Life is lived in **relationship with others**. In order to develop our own song to soar, it helps to have positive relationships with those around us, perhaps like singing in harmony within a choir. If our lives are discordant with those around us, it can be hard to sing a song to make us soar.

No-one is an island, living totally alone with no relationships, unless, you choose to live the life of a hermit, a Robinson Crusoe, or a desert father, on an island or in the middle of the desert, not relating to another human soul.

Although those days even if one chooses to live alone on an island, or away from civilisation in a desert, there will still be times of relating to others in order to say buy food and other essentials. So positive relationships are still helpful.

Positive attitude with **positive reinforcement**, can work well when looking for the best in others, and **calling out their best behaviour**.

A positive attitude can change how we think and feel about those around us. The responses given to the other person can make a change to their response.

People around us can't be changed, and mostly they can't make us do or feel anything (unless imprisoned and even then we can change our attitude to cope better and perhaps be treated better). But our attitude and positive responses can in turn affect the way others treat us in return.

If others are **treated with kindness and respect**, then they are more likely to **treat us the same way**. But if they don't treat us respectfully, their bad behaviour can be called out, in a calm but firm way.

Relationships can flourish with good communication that is **respectful and caring**. But this means that disrespectful attitudes need to be called out, without joining in with the disrespectful ways. Keeping integrity by staying calm and kind. But also being firm as to what is acceptable and not acceptable behaviour. This means to expect kindness back, while keeping calm in this exchange.

For example, if the other person is becoming heated or angry with their words, stay calm, not getting heated back. Perhaps calming say: *Let's talk about this later when we are not feeling so tired.* Then wait for a better time, like after a nice dinner with nothing else to rush to, then open the conversation, perhaps with something positive first, then bring up the subject from before, but without any derisive words or complaints. Maybe something like: *Let's talk about what we need to discuss. I was thinking perhaps we could ... What do you think?*

I remember when I was working in private practice being told a few times, to be careful not to be alone with clients who are volatile and quick to anger. I assure them that I will be fine. If I treat the client with respect, and **stay calm and kind**, then the client **tends to stay calm too**. Even if they arrive feeling angry, if I stay calm and kind, but show that I have firm boundaries, expecting them to behave in the same way, that is usually enough. A calm presence can usually de-escalate any tension.

If kindness and a calm attitude is shown to others, it makes it easier for the other person to respond in the same way.

RESPECTFUL RELATIONSHIPS

Commentary on friendship in Book of Job:
Habel, N. (1977). 'Only the jacket is my friend':
On friends and redeemers in Job.
Interpretation: A Journal of Bible & Theology, 31, 3.

2.2 Appreciating life and work

Appreciative Inquiry
Concept by Prof David Cooperrider, organisational psychologist

Steps of the appreciative inquiry approach typically include selecting a positive topic to:

(1) **Discover** and appreciate *the best of what is*

(2) **Dream** and envision *what could be*

(3) **Design** and co-construct *what should be*

(Ludema, Cooperrider, & Barrett, 2001).

Appreciative inquiry theory has been developed by organisational psychologists, as a way of encouraging positive critical by participants to brainstorm ways to transform human systems and human relationships. It refers to the power of the unconditional positive, to creatively envision ways to enhance a workplace or the wider world.

Other problem-based approaches to organisational life were finding that participants were de-energised and discouraged from the process, just thinking of more and more problems. However, with appreciative inquiry, it can be a way to approach organisational life inquiries in a more positive way, to find common visions and common values to build upon. An appreciative inquiry approach deals with ways, to explore together, the best ways forward to improve communication for a shared vision.

An appreciative inquiry approach, affirms and appreciates the visions of participants, by affirming and developing participants' ideas for social transformation.

In my own PhD research with vulnerable youth groups, this positive, appreciative, strength-based approach provided a constructive framework for youth identity affirmation activities and discussions, to promote a sense of community within the membership of the participating group. Further to the discussions of personal interests, issues of mutual interest and concern for local community issues are explored.

The appreciative question asked in my research was about what participants can creatively do to make their local community a better place. Participants explored dreams and created ideas of how they would like their future to be. This appreciative dreaming can be accomplished in supportive group work using various activities.

The community concerns were then researched in order to plan and implement community projects of their choice. The participant-led affirmative community projects with community partners can provide a means for participants to begin to experience a sense of community connectedness.

This appreciative inquiry approach, can be **adapted** to work with **personal relationship** issues, to:

***Discover** and appreciate the best of the other
***Dream** of ways to envision more of the best
***Design** specific ways to improve the relationship

This appreciative approach can help to improve relationships for each to develop a song to soar in life
(see worksheet over page for more)

Appreciative Inquiry Model
https://organizingengagement.org/about/
Prof David Cooperrider handbooks
Cooperrider, D. L., Whitney, D., & Stavros, J. M. (2003). Appreciative inquiry handbook: The first in a series of AI workbooks for leaders of change. Berrett-Koehler Publishers

See publications on **Dr Julie Morsillo PhD research**
Morsillo, J & Fisher, A. (2009). "Appreciative inquiry with migrant youth for meaningful community projects." Book chapter in M. F. Hindsworth and T. B. Lang (Eds). *Community Participation and Empowerment*. Nova Publishers.

Morsillo, J & Fisher, A. (2007). Appreciative inquiry with youth to create meaningful community projects. The Australian Community Psychologist, 19, pp.47;61.

Morsillo, J., & Prilleltensky, I. (2007). Social action with youth: Interventions, evaluation and psycho-political validity. Journal of Community Psychology, 35, pp.725;740.

Morsillo, J. (2004). Social action drama with same-sex attracted youth. The Community Psychologist, Summer 2004, 11;12.

Worksheet P — Appreciative Inquiry

Adapted for relationships

APPRECIATE what ATTRACTED you to the other (such as funny, friendly, creative, inspiring)

RE-DISCOVER what you like BEST about the other (such as faithful, reliable, carefree, supportive)

Prompts
Relationships can be difficult to manage.
We often dwell on the differences and problems and we can forget to appreciate what is good and life-giving about our relationships.
So take time to recall what you first liked about the person and the relationship and what they bring to the relationship at their best. Call out this best behaviour (positive reinforcement) to help bring out more of this good behaviour appreciating and affirming the good.

Note: This can be helpful to do before calling out the difficult or bad behaviour, so the relationship has something to build upon first.

DREAM about what you like to do together (such as exploring, travelling, times with friends)

DESIGN ways forward for the relationship (such as specific plans to do more dream times)

Consider the DESTINY the relationship could have (such as a long-term meaningful partnership)

-

Dr Julie Morsillo PhD research article
Morsillo, J & Fisher, A. (2007). Appreciative inquiry with youth to create meaningful community projects. *The Australian Community Psychologist*, 19, pp.47;61.

Appreciative Inquiry presentation
A skeptic's guide to Appreciative inquiry
by Jane Bavineau (2018)
www.youtube.com/watch?v=UfUm-6K1DRA

2.3 Communicating positively well

Communication at home and work
Helpful hints

*Be **affirming** and kind
*Compliment and **thank** any positive actions or attitudes *eg, faithfulness, working hard, roles*
*Stay **calm** - no yelling or swearing - if starting to feel frustrated or angry, calmly suggest to talk about it later when both feeling better
*Clear **boundaries** & expectations *eg clear about what you will and won't do*
*Give **generously** to home life,
 but *ask others to do their part*
*Ask for **help** if unwell or overtired
*Give the other person **time** to respond
*Be prepared to **negotiate**
*Make **suggestions** rather than demands
*Consider your **needs** and other's needs
***Share** the load within reason
*Plan outings and **holidays** within budget
*Plan times for **self** within reason
*Call out **disrespect** and bad behaviour
Use **humour or lightness when possible*
***Postpone** big or hard decisions until both not too tired or stressed
Timing - when both **relaxed if possible*
*If argument developing can stop
 eg. suggest: both tired, let's talk later
*Give each other **space** to recover from tense times

Conflict management
- Clearly, kindly and calmly state case
- Stay calm - no raised or angry voice
- Be polite - firm but kind
- Be prepared with timing when both calm

I statements (not you) - with no blame
Specific - not global, like always, every time
Pick just one issue to confront, but don't raise past

If raising an issue, give positive comments first
(i.e. What you do like, before what you don't like)

- No ultimatum or blackmail
- No negative names or swearing
- No old grievances
- Don't raise your voice
- Don't raise the stakes
- Apologise for your part

(even if seems mainly the other person's fault)

Time with challenging family hints
1. Keep contact times '**short and sweet**', trying to keep calm and kind. Don't buy into distressing issues. Don't let the awkward conversations go on for too long.

2. Have **conversation ideas** ready on topics that both can cope with, so when difficult conversations start, just **calmly change the topic** to a manageable one, like: I need to tell you a funny story about the kids or whatever.

3. Have an **exit plan** ready if you become too distressed, like politely say: I need to go now, as I'm not feeling well (and you won't be feeling well by then).

Helping family and friends in need
1. Be generous with in-kind support
- Cooking foods, take-away or going out to dinners so body and soul feel fed
- Offer to go shopping with them and pay for food and clothes if appropriate
- Offer pre-paid phone cards or whatever

2. Assist with other supports
- Community support like Centrelink or services or supported housing
- Offer help with needs, like dentist

3. Consider restricting money if concerned about illicit drugs or gambling that could cause harm

SHARE

KINDNESS

Respectful relationships
Victorian whole school programs:
Respectful Relationships promotes respect and gender equality and helps students learn how to build healthy relationships. It prepares students to face challenges by developing problem-solving skills and building resilience and confidence.

Victorian Dept of Education
Respectful relationships in schools
www.vic.gov.au/respectful-relationships

Worksheet Q – Communicating Well

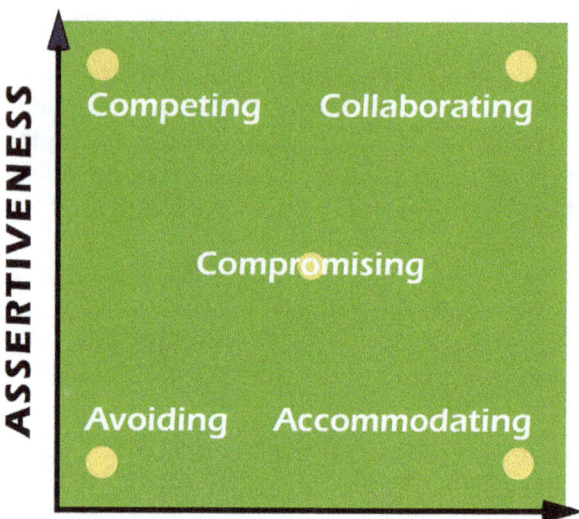

Thomas-Kilmann Conflict Mode Instrument
Copyright © 2009–2024 by Kilmann Diagnostics LLC. All rights reserved. Original figure is available at:
www.kilmanndiagnostics.com/overview-thomas-kilmann-conflict-mode-instrument-tki

What communication style do you often use? Give a typical example.

Prompts
Communication can be tricky and we can fall into habits that are not very helpful at times.
We can also give the same response to issues that have not worked well in the past.
So it can be helpful to take time to consider and practice different responses.
This might in turn, elicit a better response.

Consider other ways to communicate that might be more helpful. Write an example.

Practice what else you can do to stay calm and communicate better, such as:

_____

Breath deeply & stay calm

Plan to confront issues when calm

Affirm positive acts first

Be specific and current

Keep it short and sweet

_____

Note: We can't make another person change behaviours
But we can **respond differently** to hopefully
Improve communication and improve the outcome.

Caution: If there **is concern about any coercive control** (see next section), then couples counselling it not recommended, as this could cause more harm.

Dr Ralph H Kilmann website
See Thomas-Kilmann Conflict Mode
https://kilmanndiagnostics.com/overview-thomas-kilmann-conflict-mode-instrument-tki/

2.4 The Shark Cage – disrespectful relationships

Disrespectful relationships

All relationships need to be respectful with no coercive control, including not isolating a close friend or partner, from other friends and family.

Women often need support to recognise when boundaries are violated, especially if they have been abused as children, where they had no understanding or ability to set firm boundaries.

Women who have been abused in the part, often need support to recognise and beware of red flags in close relationships.

Red flags like:
– *'love bombing'* with constant charming comments
– discouraging spending time with others
– insisting on spending all free time together
– surveillance on where the other person
– checking who you are socialising with
– treating and talking about family members (esp mother & sisters) disrespectfully
– belittling family and friends
– finding fault with clothes, cooking, interests
– reacting badly when say 'no' to suggestions
– quick to anger and escalate disagreement
– take financial control
– physically aggressive or intimidating
– gaslighting

Women need to learn to call out bad or disrespectful behaviours of coercive control in their partners. This needs to be done with a calm and respectful attitude, so as not to escalate the violence.

Note: But not thinking they need to keep submitting to disrespectful behaviours, and constantly be forgiving bad behaviours, since that usually means no positive change and can even mean an escalation of the bad behaviour. Often it takes support to change the response and hopefully help change the behaviour of the other.

The Shark Cage
Concept by Ursula Benstead

'The Shark Cage' is a trauma informed program of interventions designed to heal and empower women who have experienced repeated abuse such as family violence and/or sexual assault. It is based on a metaphor which forms the first step in the framework. The metaphor relates to women having a high risk of male violence due to social practices that have not given girls and women the same rights as men. A consequence of this gender inequity is that some men abuse their power and violate the rights of women. It draws on a human rights approach in assisting girls and women to develop or regain a sense of their rights. It can be used by helping professionals in individual or group settings (Benstead, 2011).

Ursula Benstead Article
Benstead, U. (2011). "The Shark Cage": The Use of Metaphor with Women Who Have Experienced Abuse. *Psychotherapy in Australia,* 17(2), 70–76.

Ursula Benstead website & manual
www.thesharkcage.com
The Shark Cage manual
www.ursulabenstead.com.au/about-the-shark-cage/

Ursula Benstead interview
The Shark Cage metaphor & framework (2021)
www.youtube.com/watch?v=QW7kqvY4ruw

Coercive control

Coercive control is when someone uses patterns of abusive behaviour against another person. Over time, this creates fear and takes away the person's freedom and independence. This dynamic almost always underpins family and domestic violence.

Some signs of coercive control

- Isolating from family and friends and cultural practices
- Monitoring and controlling movements
- Monitoring or controlling finances
- Criticising or belittling behaviours and actions
- Manipulating parenting arrangements
- Threatening and intimidating behaviours
- Forcing sex

What is Coercive Control?
Desert Blue Connect, Geraldton, WA (2024)
https://desertblueconnect.org.au/what-is-coercive-control/

What is coercive control?
SBS video (2021)
www.sbs.com.au/news/video/what-is-coercive-control/52py6gjp7

Power and Control wheel (Duluth Model)
Domestic Abuse Intervention Programs (2024)
www.theduluthmodel.org

What is coercive control in domestic violence relationships?
ABC News video (2021)
www.youtube.com/watch?v=lMPh6dcvMtY

Worksheet R — Coercive Control

Consider an issue where you don't feel any control, at home or work, such as:

_____

Isolated from family & friends

Belittled regularly

Pressured to perform better

No control over finances

Little time for yourself

_____

Think of ways to address this issue, whilst protecting yourself from further harm.

Prompts

We can find ourselves feeling overwhelmed by the negative ways we are, or have been, treated by those around us. This might be subtle or indirect, or overt gaslighting. Also, the other person might be charming in public, but different in private. Plus, they might be isolating you from family and friends, so you feel you have little support.

We need to learn to call out negative or belittling behaviours, or lack of support behaviours. However, this needs to be done calmly and in a reasonable way, at a time that is not rushed or already filled with anger. It can be good to practice first, and make sure it is not likely to escalate any anger or cause unsafe behaviours. Try to choose a time when tensions are not already too high. Be calm and kind, but firm, letting them know your boundaries, that bad behaviour cannot be tolerated.

What is coercive control?
Domestic Violence explained
Adele Sheridan-Magro, St Vincent's Hospital Sydney (2023)
https://dvac.org.au/resources/information-about-domestic-and-family-violence/

NOTE: Keep in mind that when someone is very critical or angry towards you, often they are frustrated and angry about life and just taking it out on you. Try not to take it personally. Try to understand where they are coming from and help them to understand, if they are open to suggestions.

2.5 Power Threat Meaning Framework

Concept by Dr Lucy Johnstone & Dr Mary Boyle of British Psychological Society (2018)

Some British psychologists are rejecting the medical model to address mental health issues, that places the problem and the blame on the individual who is suffering. Rather, they suggest addressing the community threats and power relations that affect those suffering, and address those powerful and threatening issues or people, adversely affecting their mental health and sense of wellbeing.

Respectful relationships with no coercive control, no threats or power domination.

British Psychological Society promotes the **Power Threat Meaning Framework,** where you find out the threat on a person by someone or some system that has power over them, to work out how to overcome the threat and find meaning in their lives. Redemptive values for respectful relationship **redemptive stories** - in all aspects of our lives - being compassionate in all we do, living out our beliefs and values for respectful loving equal relationships of compassion.

Dr Lucy Johnstone & Dr Mary Boyle book
Johnson, L. & Boyle, M. (2018). *The power threat meaning framework: Overview.* British Psychological Society.

Power Threat Meaning Framework online resource
www.bps.org.uk/member-networks/division-clinical-psychology/power-threat-meaning-framework

Power Threat Meaning Framework
Webinar by Dr Lucy Johnstone
www.youtube.com/watch?v=WXrHGxVJSng

Fundamental aspects of the emergence of mental distress, with unusual experiences and problematic behaviour, can happen as follows:

1. The operation of **power** – embodied power; coercive control or power by force; legal power; economic and material power; social and cultural capital; interpersonal power; and ideological power.

2. The kinds of **threat** that the negative operation of power may pose to the individual, the group and the community, with particular reference to mental distress.

3. The central role of **meaning** – as produced within social and cultural discourses, and primed by evolved and acquired bodily responses – in shaping the operation, experience and expression of power, threat, and our responses to threat.

4. The evolved and learned **threat responses**, mediated through meaning – based bodily capabilities, that any individual – or family, group or community – experiencing threat arising within the Power Threat Meaning process, may need to use to protect themselves.

The Power Threat Meaning Framework replaces the question: What is wrong with you?' with four key questions:

1. 'What has happened to you?'
   (How is **power** operating in your life?)

2. 'How did it affect you?'
   (What kind of **threats** does this pose?)

3. 'What sense did you make of it?'
   (What is the **meaning** of these situations and experiences to you?)

4. 'What did you have to do to survive?'
   (What kinds of **threat response** are you using?)
Translated into practice with an individual, family or group, two additional questions need to be asked:

5. 'What are your strengths?'
   (What access to **power resources** do you have?)

6. ...and to integrate all the above:
   'What is your story?' (p.190)

Worksheet S – Power Threat Meaning Framework

1. What has happened to you?
   (How in power operating in your life?)

   ----

2. How did this affect you?
   (What threats does this pose?)

   ----

3. What sense did you make of it?
   (What is the meaning of these experiences to you?)

   ----

4. What have you done to survive?
   (What are your threat responses?)

   ----

5. 'What are your strengths?'
   (What access to power resources do you have?)

   ----

6. 'What is your story?'

Prompt
We can have times in our lives when we feel overwhelmed by a powerful person or system, that makes us feel threatened. These powerful threats can still influence us from any childhood experiences. As a child, we often have very limited choices in our responses, feeling silenced or not listened too. So when threated as an adult, sometimes we revert to a similar response as a child. However, as adults we do have more choices and more supports, to help up stand up to threatening powerful people or systems. We just need support to recall what we have done well, and to work out the best ways to respond, to negotiate or leave (temporarily or permanently) the situation. We can work towards the best ways forward, to help create a song to sing and soar in life.

Power Threat Meaning Framework webinar
by Dr Lucy Johnstone (2023)
www.youtube.com/watch?v=WXrHGxVJSng

2.6 Dealing with difficult relationships

Practical hints learnt from my sister

Two concepts that might be helpful to consider when spending time with family members whom they find difficult to deal with, and to protect themselves:

1. Keep contact times '**short and sweet**', trying to keep calm, but have an exit plan ready if you become too distressed, like politely say: *I need to go now, as I'm not feeling well* (and you probably won't be feeling well. by then)

2. Have conversation ideas ready on topics that you can both cope with, so when difficult conversations start, just **calmly change the topic** to a manageable one, like: *Let's not talk about that now. I need to tell you a funny story about the kids or whatever.*

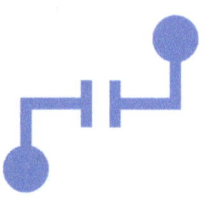

More practical hints
Dr John Gottman & Dr Julie Gottman
Healthy relationships research & advice
www.gottman.com

The science of love – Ted Talk
by Dr John Gottman (2018)
www.youtube.com/watch?v=-uazFBCDvVw

Improving relationships
Active Constructive Responding by Prof Shelly Gable

Prof Shelly Gable and her team theorised and examined the ways of responding to good news and found that people most commonly respond to good news in one of **four** way:

Passive Destructive – responding with disinterest, does not pay much attention, changes the topic of conversation.

Passive Constructive – passively engaged with little enthusiasm and doesn't make a big deal of the situation

Active Destructive – actively points out the problems associated with the 'good' news, creates doubt and concern about the scenario, completely kills any excitement

Active Constructive – actively responds to the good news with interest and enthusiasm, asks questions that help to almost re-experience the moment, the conversation is a pleasant and joyful one for both participants.

When a friend, colleague or loved one shares the gift of good news, it's our initial response to what is being shared, that can directly contribute to the building and maintenance of healthy, happy relationships.

Prof Shelly Gable on Active Constructive Responding
Gable, S. L., Gonzaga, G. C., & Strachman, A. (2006). Will you be there for me when things go right? Supportive responses to positive event disclosures. *Journal of Personality and Social Psychology, 91*(5), 904-917.

Active & Constructive Responding
by Social Skills Coaching (2024)
www.youtube.com/watch?v=X1UxnMv2BRg

Fly away song

        Poem by Dr Julie Morsillo, 1999

Written when I thought I might have
to make significant changes in my life

Flying here, flying there,
searching everywhere
Following our dreams
following our dreams

Flying in from exotic isle
So young and so innocent
Staying with friends in a narrow hall
With dreams waiting a call.

Hearing your music playing
A sweet Gaelic melody
'Morning has broken like the first morn'
T'was love at first sound

Singing my songs so full of promise
You composing the haunting tunes
Dancing our dreams making music together
All the day long

Journeying far from our friends and family
For a new life to fulfil
Discovered a home in a castle on the hill
High above the sea

Studied hard thirsting for knowledge
Weaving our dreams in the web of life
Walking along the glittering sea shore
Captured the tune that we had longed for

Settling in a new home, creating a family
Developing our own community
Opening our lives to welcome others in
Opening up our home

Taking in the friendless children
So alone in the great wide world
Sharing our lives for a little while
To make a life of their own

Venturing out to the larger community
To save some souls from this world of woe
The challenge was great to do our part
To do our small part

Flying high was our next adventure
Far far away over the sea
Immersed in many exotic cultures
With magical history

Now is the time for another dream
To keep travelling along the beam
We'll search afar to follow the star
To follow the star.

2.7 Respectful relationships stories

Gift of friendship
by Laura Boys, 2021.

It is the greatest gift
To let tears wash off your makeup
A hug brush off the mask of "I'm okay"
And concerned eyes bare open your aching heart.

It is the greatest gift
To hear a laugh at your joke
Have a cup of coffee paid for
And a companion for every adventure

It is the greatest honour
To share your tears in mournful silence
Offer a hug to someone who needs it
And look with empathy at an aching soul

It is the greatest honour
To laugh at another's joke
Pay for someone's coffee
And be asked to join an adventure.

It is the greatest gift to have a friend
It is the greatest honour to be a friend.

Skills for healthy romantic relationships
By Dr Joanne Davila (2015)
www.youtube.com/watch?v=gh5VhaicC6g

Establishing boundaries in relationships
by Mary Hoang, psychologist (2021)
www.youtube.com/watch?v=8WCVJJfTLAU

Meditation Steps:

Begin this meditation by finding a comfortable space away from distraction and responsibility.

Take three deep mindful breaths, concentrating on the feeling of air expanding your belly as you inhale and the belly releasing as you exhale.
Begin to focus on a close friend. Picture them as vividly as you can in your mind and focus on all their most beautiful qualities.

Encourage these feelings of love to grow by using imagery such as picturing your heart as a candle and the light and warmth growing until it reaches all the way to your friend's heart. You can also repeat phrases such as "may you feel loved, cared for and accepted" or "may you feel happy, content and at peace."

The second aspect is to think of someone you have neutral feelings toward such as an acquaintance. This focus on expressing care towards everyday people fosters a sense of shared humanity and empathy toward people who might be experiencing their own stories of hardship.

After meditating on your close friend, expand this feeling of love toward an acquaintance that you neither like or dislike.

Kindness to a friend mediation:
Compassion Focused Therapy
by Lewis Psychology – 10 mins (2020)
www.youtube.com/watch?v=yr6TZE6XTg4

2.8 Biography and Dignity Therapy

Biography therapy in palliative care
Concept by Dr Ivan Lichter, New Zealand surgeon, 1993

Volunteers help patients to tell of their significant memories for a written memoirs as legacy for family

Diagnosis of a life-limiting disease is a disruptive experience. In consequence patients often feel that life is divided in the time before diagnosis and the time with the illness. Patients need to cope with their illness and need to realign their identity accordingly. Palliative care is a **holistic approach**, with all health care professionals in the team in **close communication** with the patient and their caregivers looking for resources supporting the patient. Narratives are an important tool to construct meaning, and there is a growing body of literature and research in the use of narratives in palliative care. Telling stories is an intrinsic part of human beings. An alleviating effect may be achieved by a nonjudgmental and interested listener. Volunteers` engagement with patients to **ask for significant moments in their life stories that they can leave as a legacy** to the family and friends.

Different concepts using biographical elements have been proposed such as Short-Term Life Review, Life Review, Life Completion Therapy, Meaning-Making Intervention, Living with Hope Program, or Dignity Therapy.

Biography Therapy article
Lichter I, Mooney J, Boyd M.(1993). Biography as therapy. Palliative Medicine Research, 7(2):133-7.

Biography Therapy volunteering
Volunetering program in Melbourne (2024)
www.epc.asn.au/news/epc-has-published-over-1500-biographies-_117s121

Dignity Therapy book
Chochinov, H.M. (2012) *Dignity therapy: Final words for final days.* Oxford University Press.

Dignity therapy in palliative care
Concept by Dr Harvey Chochinov, Canadian surgeon, 2021

Dignity Therapy is an intervention for people facing serious illness, focuses on dignity conservation tasks such as settling relationships, sharing words of love, and preparing a legacy document for loved ones.

Chochinov proposed Dignity Therapy as a psychotherapeutic intervention for people facing serious illness. It focuses on dignity conservation tasks such as settling relationships, sharing words of love, and preparing legacies of memory and shared values, all of which take on a heightened importance at the end of life. Perceiving that dignity depends on experiences of generativity and the pursuit of purpose and meaning, Chochinov identified aspects of dignity-conserving care and proposed a model for its development, study, and use by clinicians to promote maintenance of dignity for patients facing serious illness. This model includes spiritual as well as psychosocial and physical elements.

Dignity question for each person entering palliative care is:
*What do I need to know about you to give you the best care possible?

Dr. Chochinov and his colleagues developed a manualized guide for Dignity therapy. The intervention uses 10 core questions that guide an interview, including:

- What are your most important accomplishments, and what do you feel most proud of?
- What are your hopes and dreams for your loved ones?
- What have you learned about life that you would want to pass along to others?

End-of-life care using dignity therapy:

- Writing memoirs as a legacy or
- Writing a letter to close (or estranged) relative or friend as a legacy (see more over page).

Worksheet T — Dignity Therapy

What do others need to know about you to give you the best care when you are unwell or in care?

What story would you like others to remember you by? What legacy would you like to leave for the family?

Prompts
More creative ideas for working with the elderly

Photo album booklet
Take photos of elderly person's favourite photos that they might have in their room or home to make up a booklet with a phrase or sentence about each photo, from what they have told you. This can be a keep-sake for them and their relatives. Also, to share with them, more positive stories about their life and remember the redemptive stories, their stories to soar again.

Picture booklet
Ask about where they have lived and enjoyed visiting in their travels. If they don't have photos, look up any pictures online that they might relate too, and print out the ones that resonate with them, to make a booklet with a phrase or sentence about each picture. Another way to share positive enriching stories, their redemptive stories, their stories to soar again.

Write a letter or thank you card
Ask if they might want to write a letter to a relative (or friend), or dictate a letter for you to write in their behalf. This could be to someone that they would like to repair their relationship with. Alternatively, they might want to thank someone that has been particularly caring or worked particularly hard for them or others, to show appreciation and feel better.

Dignity Therapy in palliative care in Australia
https://palliativecare.org.au/story/talking-about-your-life-can-help-the-process-of-accepting-death/

Dr Harvey Chochinov presentation
Dignity at the end of life (2023)
www.youtube.com/watch?v=hA0YP4QJJd4

Part 3 – **A** supportive community encircling us

Peace Song

Song by Dr Julie Morsillo, 1984

Peace for a world that is crying
Peace is the cry
Peace for a world that needs harmony
Yet it starts with me

Peace I need within myself
Not quick to anger
Befriending all
Looking for good…

DO JUSTLY
LOVE MERCY
WALK HUMBLY
Micah 6:8

Peace we need with family
Not causing strife
Working as one
To see justice done…

Peace we need over the earth
Not kill a one
Turning from hate
Come to unity …

Peace for a world that is crying
Peace is the cry
Peace for a world that needs harmony
Yet it starts with me

3.1 Caring community services

Feeling safe and supported

To feel safe and supported, encircled by a compassionate community, where each **feels valued** in order to **add value** to the community (Prilleltensky, 2014). Compassionate community groups to show care, and services provided by government and non-government agencies, to provide good healthcare and education, and the means to acquire housing that is safe and supported.

Provision of adequate community services for a sense of wellbeing:

– Health care that is accessible and affordable with doctors and community health services

– Educational pathways that are local, including neighbourhood houses, TAFE, online courses

– Housing that is available and affordable, including crisis housing, supported housing

– Transport with concessions for public transport.

Everyone needs a safe and supportive community with adequate health care, education, housing and transport, for a sense of wellbeing. Local councils and state government websites can offer services. **Local community health care centres and local neighbourhood houses** can offer much support too. This can all help to develop a song to sing to soar in life.

Sense of community article
McMillan, D. W. (1996). Sense of community. *Journal of Community Psychology*, 24, 4, 315-325.

What is sense of community? Community Psychology
by Erika Sanbourne Media LLC Animated video (2021)
www.youtube.com/watch?v=Moa943MVQWg

Neighbourhood Day: Creating a sense of community
Video by Port Adelaide Enfield City Council (2022)
www.youtube.com/watch?v=qvOSplLWx9Q

Figure 2: Cycle for life by Dr Julie Morsillo & Laura Boys 2022

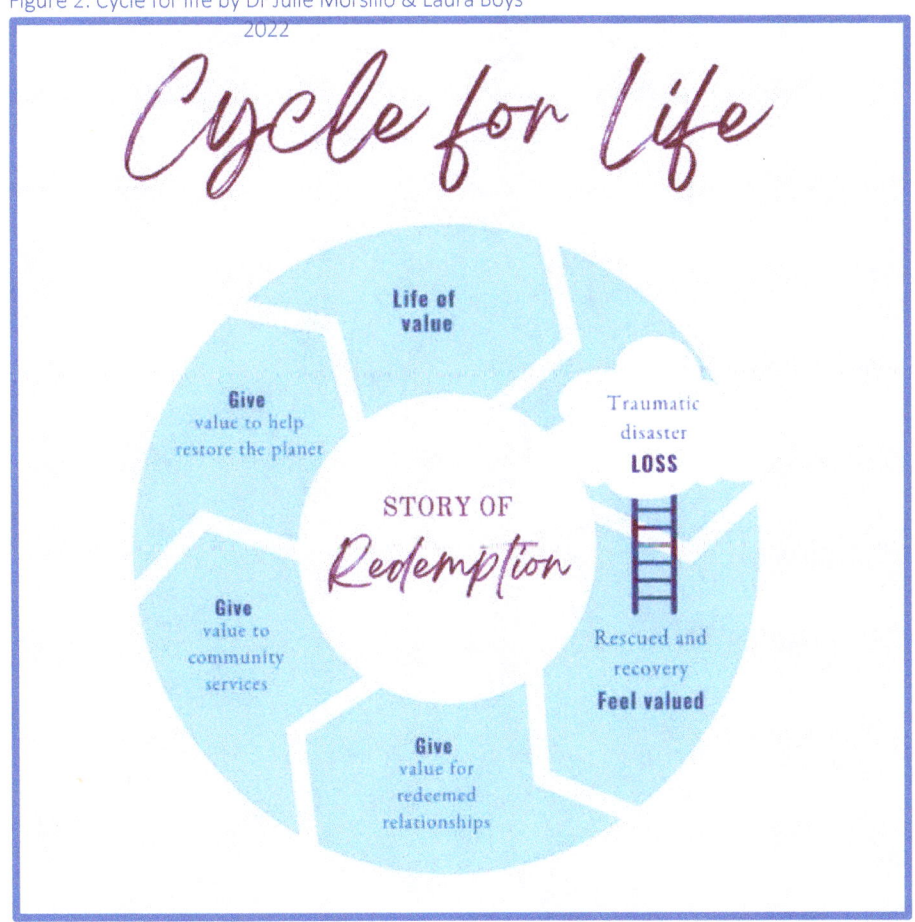

Song for community
Song by Dr Julie Morsillo, lockdowns in 2020

This is the day we will sing
this is the day we will shout
We will have our freedom one day
to leave our homes, to meet again

We have a common cause,
a shared struggle, to defeat the virus
A worldwide cause like we have had before
An intimate disaster to rally to a cause

We have had climate change
with oceans filled with plastics
Islands and coastlands
disappearing with tsunamis
Droughts taking away arid lands
causing wars of desperation

We have had worldwide disasters
 and wars before
Fire to destroy our lands and homes
with smoke to fill our lungs
Yet we still could not work together well globally

Now we are rallying as a global community
So save our souls from the virus
To protect our vulnerable
and protect our economy

Our governments are finding their hearts
Giving to those in need,
not just lining the pockets of the rich
We are seeing kindness in the policies
and kindness in the shops
Kindness in places where we have
not seen much before

So when the virus is gone, we will sing and shout
We will care for each other and care for our plant
Think beyond ourselves and just our own needs
Love our neighbour, love our planet

We will sing, we will shout, we will care,
We will care for each other and care for our plant
This is the day we look forward too

Free to enjoy each other's company
Hugging each other and hugging our planet
To protect from further harm

Song of Community Tune
Inspired by Waltz of the Flowers
Nutcracker Ballet by Pyotr Ilyich Tchaikovsky
New York City Ballet (2020)
www.youtube.com/watch?v=LKcZL8q1eBw

Worksheet U – Community Supports

What community supports do you have or would like to have, that you value? This could be:

Safe environment

Adequate housing

Good health care services

Time for rest and relaxation

Accessible educational pathways

Supportive faith or family community

Trees and parklands in neighbourhood

Prompts

We all need support from others at times. Particularly those new to the country, moved recently, or with health issues. Practical support in needed: with safe affordable housing, available health care services, suitable educational pathways and care in the home as appropriate.

Emotional support is needed: with friendships, through family, carers, religious or sports communities, and other community groups and services. We need to check that the person in need, does have adequate community services and community groups for friendship and care. This can help with a song to sing and soar in life.

Community health services in Victoria
www.health.vic.gov.au/community-health/community-health-services

Community-led support for refugees in Australia
Video by Community Refugee Sponsorship Aust (2021)
www.youtube.com/watch?v=nvpAHpAczdA

Stronger together:
Loneliness & Social connectedness in Australia
Bankwest Curtin Economics Centre panel (2021)
www.youtube.com/watch?v=aN3u24Bxwk4

Improve mental health with art & fitness
ABC Australia Backroads in Pinnaroo SA (2022)
www.youtube.com/watch?v=hhqmgIRLRmM

3.2 Meaningful community groups

We need communities of support around us, from extended families to faith-communities or movement communities or creative communities, to provide support and life-giving creativity and compassion.

Extended family & friends – own tribe

It can be good to have extended families with aunts and uncles, cousins and grandparents, who know and love us well (even if they send us crazy at times!). Or if no extended family nearby, then friends from our neighbourhoods and local community groups, who do live near us, and have some similar interests and similar family issues. Sometimes, local communities can be there to support us in times of need and also to celebrate good times together too, where they become like family to us.

Some families have rituals, like bowing heads and saying or singing a grace, before main meals with hands together in supplication, or just saying a kind word to those who prepared the meal – We are very grateful for this food.

The Great Synagogue, Prague

Faith-based & spiritual communities

It can be life-giving, to have communities with similar ethos to us, to support us with kindness and generosity. Faith-based communities, at their best, can offer generosity to each other, and care of each other in times of need, supporting each other with loving kindness.

Religious communities often create sacred spaces in dedicated places. Sacred religious spaces, can come in many forms, including cathedrals, mosques and synagogues. These sacred places can be for quiet contemplation, away from every-day life, with guided meditation, using symbols, icons, candles, and such, to reflect on the goodness we have in life, and kindnesses we can give to others in the community.

Sacred spaces with sacred rituals can provide time for an enhanced community life. For example, regular Christian church worship services, taking time out from the busyness of daily life, to come together as a community, with symbols and rituals to reflect on the sacredness of life, with its suffering and service. We can gather to pray and support each other as a community, for comfort, and for courage to go back into the world, and care for those in need and care for the world around us, to make this world a better place.

These religious symbols can remind us to value ourselves and value others with compassion, for a more caring community and caring world that benefits us all.

Many forms of meaningful community groups

Meaningful community groups come in all shapes and forms, to benefit our well-being, to develop a song to sing and soar. This can include:

Groups promoting physical health
– Sports and fitness clubs – keep fit and socialise
– Yoga, Tai Chi, Pilates – for core strength

Groups promoting creativity
– Creative arts and crafts and art therapy
– Music groups and community choirs
– (see Seeking harmony by Brunswick Women's Choir)
– Book clubs and creative interest groups
– Men's shed with woodworking or repairing

Clubs promoting connection with nature
– Walking, bushwalking, hiking, tramping
– Boating and fishing,
– Snorkelling and diving
– Community gardens
– Connecting with nature (see next section)

Support groups - for mental health & wellbeing issues
– Support group for grieving a loved one
– Alcoholics Anonymous (AA),
– Narcotics Anonymous (NA)
– Support groups for family & friends of those struggling
  with mental health and wellbeing issues

SEEKING HARMONY
Stories from the Brunswick Women's Choir

Seeking harmony:
Stories from the Brunswick Women's Choir
Catriona Milne & BWC History Book editorial committee (2006) Brunswick Women's Choir.

Brunswick Women's Choir video (2018)
www.youtube.com/watch?v=ZyTW5J9sDOs

Creating sacred spaces
Creating sacred spaces for ourselves and for those in need, with the sacred pastoral spaces, spaces in counselling rooms, with no judgement, only empathy, with a listening ear, sharing values of compassion and care for the other.

Sacred spaces can also be found in nature, with walking and enjoying: bushwalking, beach, rivers, mountains, and any place of beauty from natural creation. (More in final section).

Supportive community stories
The recognition of marginalised people is so important for a supportive community. **Speak**ing up for those who are different, and supporting others to do the same.

Celebrating diversity can help build supportive communities. Like appreciating different cultural foods and festivals to add more positive experiences to our lives, while bringing people together. This develops positive community narratives.

Community narratives, are made up of similar personal stories, that equally become the foundation of a community identity (Rappaport, 2000).

My story from Brunswick Women's Choir
Many years ago, when singing in the Brunswick Women's Choir, with Cathy Nixon as director, we had the privilege of having workshops with various local migrant community groups, who were prepared to teach us some of their traditional folk songs, and the stories behind their cultural music. We performed songs in many different languages, and some local community groups even sang with us in performances. This was a great joy for us and for them. Celebrating diversity and appreciating each other's cultural diversity, gave us new songs to sing and to soar in life.

Worksheet V – Community Garden

Community garden or other community project
We're all in this together. Consider ways you could gather a community group for a specific project, such as a community garden.

How will you build a community to help care for the community garden? Here are some questions to consider:

*What skills does everyone need to learn?

*What tools are needed?

*What changes need to be made?

*How will you support each other?

Prompts
Joining or forming a community group, can increase our sense of wellbeing, social connectedness and belonging.

This community garden exercise, could be adapted to other community groups in nature, such as:
– Bushwalking group
– Local art group or craft group using things from nature
– Friends of local park or river
 (volunteers for plantings, clearing, keeping it clean)
– Transition towns with local communities helping each other to live greener and cleaner.

Loving kindness meditation on community

The third stage of the loving-kindness meditation involves further expanding the feeling of love and compassionate care toward all people throughout the world.

> Never believe that a few caring people can't change the world. For, indeed, that's all who ever have.
> Maragaret Mead

More ideas and resources for community projects:

Growing veggies and friendships video
Gardening Australia (2021)
www.youtube.com/watch?v=DtsGaaTbJ6o

Unused public space to a community farm video
Gardening Australia (2022)
www.youtube.com/watch?v=yT0FPs6dPvE

Craft group donates handmade good to vulnerable communities
ABC Australia video (2020)
www.youtube.com/watch?v=AYG-vA1xHB8

Organisations providing support to refugees
List on Common Grace (2024)
www.commongrace.org.au/organisations_supporting_asylum_seekers

Building community resilience after natural disasters
Video by Relationships Australia NSW (2023)
www.youtube.com/watch?v=WFI_Q7-IKxw

Transition towns in Australia
Inspiring and supporting local communities
To build a sustainable future
https://transitionaustralia.net

Worksheet W – Community Groups

What community groups do you have or would like to have that you value? For example, this could be:

_____

Faith-based community

Art or Craft group

Community choir

Sports group

Dance group

Book club

Community garden group

_____

Prompts
Joining or forming a community group, can increase your sense of wellbeing, social connectedness and belonging.

Here are some more examples of community groups, for creative spaces or to help others:
– Community choir or community band (or any music group)
– Neighbourhood houses with community interest groups
– Bushwalking group
– Local sports group
– Local art group or craft group
– Local op-shop volunteering
– Spiritual or religious group in person or online
– Local activist groups to stand up for a cause to improve human rights for caring communities

Neighbourhood Houses Victoria
Local community programs and activities
www.nhvic.org.au

Christian action group seeking to end inhuman treatment of asylum seekers
https://actionnetwork.org/groups/love-makes-a-way-australia

Diverse community groups in Gungahlin, Canberra
Helping newcomers forge strong connections, ABC News (2021)
www.youtube.com/watch?v=F60q1Q7LQcQ

Asylum Seeker Resource Centre volunteers
Supporting asylum seekers in Australia
https://asrc.org.au/become-a-volunteer/

Part 4 – **R**estorative time in nature

4.1 Appreciating connections to nature

Indigenous belonging to the land
Quote by Prof Pat Dodson

In the words of Indigenous leader, Pat Dodson (former Senator & former Catholic priest):

"Land is a living place.... It belongs to me, I belong to the land, I rest in it. I come from there. Land is a notion that is most difficult to categorise in English...but it provides for my physical needs and provides for my spiritual needs. It is a regeneration of stories."

See: Stockton, E. (1995). *The Aboriginal Gift: spirituality for a nation*. Millennium Books, p.82.

Indigenous peoples in Australia, have a truly spiritual connection with the land, connection to nature, to Mother Earth, that they call country.

Prof Pat Dodson lecture
The road to reconciliation (ANU, 2013)
www.youtube.com/watch?v=qPko-a1TMXk

Connecting with nature
for calm, awe, beauty and sustenance.
Caring for nature as nature cares for us,
for a song to sing and soar.

Appreciating the wonders of the world
Baird, J. (2020). *Phosphorescence: On awe, wonder and things that sustain you when the world goes dark*. Fourth Estate.

Country for life
Quote by Deborah Bird Rose, 1996

'Country is a place that gives and receives life. Not just imagined or represented, it is lived in and lived with.

Country in Aboriginal English is not only a common noun but also a proper noun. People talk about country in the same way that they would talk about a person: they speak to country, sing to country, visit country, worry about country, feel sorry for country, and long for country.

People say that country knows, hears, smells, takes notice, takes care, is sorry or happy. Country is not a generalised or undifferentiated type of place, such as one might indicate with terms like 'spending a day in the country' or 'going up the country'.

Rather, country is a living entity with a yesterday, today and tomorrow, with a consciousness, and a will toward life. Because of this richness, country is home, and peace; nourishment for body, mind, and spirit; heart's ease.'

Prof Deborah Bird Rose book
See: Rose, D.B. (1996). Nourishing Terrains: Australian Aboriginal view of landscape and wilderness.
Australian Heritage Commission.

Prof Deborah Bird Rose presentation
Country and the gift
(Sydney Environment Institute, 2014)
www.youtube.com/watch?v=suSbvoAw0g4

The beautiful connection between people and country
Back to Nature ABC iview (2021)
www.youtube.com/watch?v=DAGBVE3V4s0

4.2 Creating in nature

Community Gardens

Gardening can be for beauty and for sustenance – flowers for beauty and the for the bees, and plants for eating, to help with sustainable food security.

Community gardens are public shared spaces to primarily grow food, with produce often shared.

The concept came from Victory Gardens in USA schools and USA & Canada, to promote food gardens for every home in WW1 to help with food security. The concept was used again in USA, Britain, Germany, and Australia after WW2 in public parks and private homes for food security.

History of community gardens
https://daily.jstor.org/the-surprising-backstory-of-victory-gardens/

Artwork with nature and nature photography are other creative ways to enjoy and appreciate nature.

4.3 Restoring nature

There are many ways to support the restoring of nature, after much clearance for human habitation. This includes activities like:

- Planting trees, growing food
- Natural products, recycling, upcycling
- Clean energy like wind farms & solar energy
- Greening
- Food security
- *Small is beautiful* living

Garden project for inclusive community connection
Gardening Australia (2024)
www.youtube.com/watch?v=fyIPhREMymo

4.4 Living in nature

Time in nature to relax and be refreshed:
- Walk in parklands
- Outdoor play equipment in natural settings
- Bushwalking, hiking, tramping
- Swimming in sea or lakes
- Fishing, kayaking, boating
- Outdoor sports

Eco-villages and transition towns
Intentionally, living closer to calming and restorative nature with community support.

Transition towns
Local communities inspiring and supporting each other for a sustainable future.
transitionaustralia.net

Eco-villages
An eco-village has shared land for community gardens and community spaces for relaxation.

Eco-village, Castlemaine, Vic website
Eco-village, The Paddock, Castlemaine, Victoria, Australia
www.thepaddockcastlemaine.com.au

Eco-village Pioneers video
Permaculture Magazine (2010)
www.youtube.com/watch?v=1m5rSTVIV-A

Worksheet X — Restorative Time in Nature

How do you spend time, or would like to spend time in nature to flourish? Such as:

_____

Walk in local parklands

Run or ride in parklands

Gardening at home

Community gardening

Swimming or water aerobics

Camping

Driving through natural country
_____

Prompts

Living in an industrial world, particularly in the cities and large towns, we can become distanced from nature, from the natural Mother Earth, that gives us life. We can learn from Indigenous peoples (and farmers at times), about how to be more connected with the land and care for the land, so it cares for us.

Spending more time in nature can give us many health benefits, helping us to feel more relaxed, and calm, or even more inspired about life. So think about ways to be more connected with nature and enjoy this connection, to help develop a song to sing and soar in life.

Health benefits of nature video
Back to Nature ABC View (2021)
www.youtube.com/watch?v=19T26Qunxf8

Ecotherapy benefits article
Chaudhury, P. & Banerjee, D. (2020). "Recovering With Nature": A Review of Ecotherapy and Implications for the COVID-19 Pandemic. *Frontiers in Public Health*, 10 Dec, 2020.

4.5 Eco-therapy or nature therapy

Ecotherapy can involve loosely structured activities, such as walking along the beach or going for a hike in a forested area. You can also choose to participate in more formal approaches, often with guidance from a therapist. Some of these approaches include:

***Community gardening or farming** – Gardening with neighbours on shared land offers the chance to grow your own produce, build relationships, and spend time working outdoors. Some programs also teach basic farming tasks like tending animals or crops.

***Wilderness or adventure therapy** – This approach to mental health treatment teaches coping techniques and therapeutic skills to teens and young adults as they camp and hike in the wilderness with their peers.

***Park prescriptions** – Some healthcare providers and mental health professionals are starting to recommend that people spend a specific amount of time each week visiting a park or pursuing other outdoor activities.

***Forest bathing** – Slightly more than a walk in the park, this practice encourages the mindful use of your five senses as you ramble through forests or similarly tree-heavy settings.

***Animal-assisted therapy** – Petting, playing, or working with animals like horses, dogs, and birds outdoors can offer another way to manage stress.

***Outdoor meditation and yoga** – Yoga and meditation offer well-established benefits, but they may be even more rewarding outside.

Benefits of nature therapies can be:
*Reduces depression and anxiety
*Makes us more calm, focused and creative
*Improves our mood and sleeping habits
*Helps us to recover quicker after surgery or illness

Source: Metaphorically Speaking website

Japanese Forest Bathing
The term emerged in Japan in the 1980s as a physiological and psychological exercise called *shinrin-yoku* ("forest bathing" or "taking in the forest atmosphere"). The purpose was twofold: to offer an eco-antidote to tech-boom burnout and to inspire residents to reconnect with and protect the country's forests.

Forest bathing basics

*Find a suitable place that's easy and pleasant to walk on, has places to sit, and ideally with access to natural waterways and different aspects. It also helps if it's close to home.

*On arrival, notice the place you are in, notice your body, and tune in to your senses.

*Walk slowly with steady step-by-step pace, while silently noticing what is in motion in the forest. If you start to feel distracted or rushed, come to a complete halt.

*Make friends with the forest. Notice the trees, stones, plants and flowers. Listen to the forest. Let the natural world make an impression on your mind.

*Find a comfortable place to sit, staying still for up to 20 minutes, cultivating awareness.

*Give back. Quietly acknowledge everything the forest gives you.

Source: The Nature and Forest Therapy Association

The Japanese art of Forest Bathing
Life of Kotts (2021)
www.youtube.com/watch?v=5L8mEU4OGjs

Worksheet Y — Nature Therapy

Forest bathing basics

Find a suitable place that's easy and pleasant to walk on, has places to sit, and ideally with access to natural waterways and different aspects. It also helps if it's close to home.

On arrival, **notice the place you are in**, notice your body, and tune in to your senses.

Walk slowly with steady step-by-step pace, while silently noticing what is in motion in the forest. If you start to feel distracted or rushed, come to a complete halt.

Make friends with the forest. Notice the trees, stones, plants and flowers. Listen to the forest. Let the natural world make an impression on your mind.

Sit down. Find a comfortable place to sit, staying still for up to 20 minutes, cultivating awareness.

Give back. Quietly acknowledge everything the forest gives you

Source: The Nature and Forest Therapy Association

Nature walk with Lucy Van Sambeek (calling in distance), student Susanna in foreground, at Glomar Beach, near Seaspray, East Gippsland, Victoria, 2023.

Forest therapy Victoria website
www.foresttherapyvictoria.com.au

Nature & Forest Therapy
with Lucy Van Sambeek
www.metaphoricallyspeaking.com.au/category/nature-and-forest-therapy/

Guided parks walks in Victoria
Parks Victoria website (2024)
www.parks.vic.gov.au/healthy-parks-healthy-people/park-walks

Forest Bathing in Deep Creek National Park video
with Bronwyn Paynter, Dept of Environment & Water SA (2020)
www.youtube.com/watch?v=U344VH0pAl0

Free guided walks
Royal Botanical Gardens Victoria (Melbourne) (2024)
www.rbg.vic.gov.au/melbourne-gardens/whats-on-melbourne/free-guided-walk/

4.6 Narrative walks

Nature therapy meets narrative therapy
Concept by Chris Darmody, 2019

The concept of a narrative walk, takes the principles of nature therapy and the principles of narrative therapy, and brings them together for a time walking in nature, to not only reflect on nature, but reflect on a personal issue within the calming environment of nature.

A narrative walk can be with a group on a bushwalk to the sea or a river, and then walk back the same way (with 5 stops along the way for reflection time with paper and pen).

The distance can be adjusted for the particular group, and it works well to be in a place without too many distractions, but with a safe pathway.

A handout for participants on the walk can be provided, with space for written reflection at each stop (see worksheet over page).

Stop 1 – **Naming problem** - Select a stone, twig of leaf to represent a problem you want to consider and work through.

Stop 2 – Consider **unique outcomes** when problem was not all consuming

Stop 3 – Develop **preferred story** about the problem – some benefits or ways to cope

Throw the symbol into water before returning – as a ritual expressing out loud why you can think about it differently now

Walk back the same way.

Stop 4 – Re-thinking learnings and **personal supports** you have to develop your preferred story

Stop 5 – Consider your **personal agency** with ways to overcome the issue with own strengths and supports.

Nature walk with Andrea, Jen, Pinky & Deb, Master of Community Counselling students of Eastern College Australia, 2023.

Narrative Walks by Chris Darmody article
Darmody, C. (2019) Narrative walks. *International Narrative Therapy and Community Work*, No 1, 2019, p. 52-60.

Narrative Walks in practice
Metaphorically Speaking with Lucy Van Sambeek
www.metaphoricallyspeaking.com.au/narrative-walks/

Worksheet Z — Narrative Walk

Welcome to narrative walk in nature
Walking to a body of water,
and walking back the same way.
(long or short - as suitable for the group)

Part 1 Identify the problem
– *consider a problem to work on*
(preferably before the walk starts)
How long has the problem been around?
What can make the problem bigger?
Name the impact on your life?

Walk the first section ready to share the problem

STOP 1 *(sit on small mat provided)*
Share problem name, reflect on problem issues, and pick up a nature object to represent problem.

Part 2 Unique outcomes
When is problem strongest and weakest?
When can you challenge the problem?
What was it like with no problem?

Walk second section ready to share time when problem reduced or able to challenge the problem

STOP 2 Share unique outcomes

Part 3 Developing a preferred story
What made it possible to challenge the problem?
Does this thing have a name?
Where did this thing come from?

Walk third section ready to share a name for your strength to help challenge the problem

LUNCH STOP – *lake, river or beach*

Write a letter to problem to share, before invitation to throw nature object away.

Throw away the nature symbol of the problem.

WALK back the same way

Photo at local Queens Park Lake,
Moonee Ponds, Melbourne, 2023.

Part 4 Re-membering
Where did you learn to deal with the problem?
Any supports to overcome the problem?
What might they say now if here?

Walk fourth section (retracing steps of previous section) remembering those who helped you develop your strength

RETRACE STOP - Share supports

Part 5 Agency
What strengthening ways of overcoming problem?
What reminds to strengthen?
Who could help you to become stronger?

Final part of walk consider one thing to do after the walk & a personal letter to self.

FINAL STOP
– Share action & letter.

Walk final section back to beginning.
Step back into initial space to recognise
the beginning and end of the journey.

Narrative Walk worksheet
Prepared by Dr Julie Morsillo
Adapted from Lucy Van Sambeek
www.metaphoricallyspeaking.com.au/narrative-walks/
and adapted from original concept by Chris Darmody

Darmody, C. (2019) Narrative walks. *International Narrative Therapy and Community Work*, No 1, 2019, p. 52-60.

4.7 Restoring nature ideas

Think of some ways to enjoy nature and perhaps help to restore nature.

What can you put in place in your garden to help future generations?

How can you take care of the world's gardens?

Activities

Appreciate nature with:

- Mindful nature walks
- Spend time in your garden
- Visit beautiful places
- Create art about nature

Ideas for practical steps:

*Build a bee hotel

*Research and get involved with your local council's environmental programs

*Spread awareness of restoring nature

*Put plants in your garden that attract and provide habitats for native animals.

*Learn about sustainable living and what steps you can take to recycle and reuse more of your items.

Loving kindness meditation in nature

The last section of the loving kindness meditation involves expanding the feeling of love toward all of mother nature, of creation.

Original painting by cousin Elizabeth Ruth Stein, 2019
(formally Wendy Donellan)

Coral Reef Collage
by Zart Australia Art Activity (2023)
www.youtube.com/watch?v=khpkEiqtnDM

Australian flower garden inspires Artist-Gardener
ABC Australia Podcast (2020)
www.youtube.com/watch?v=fpf5EeQu75U

A Franciscan Blessing
A challenge to care for those in need.
by Sister Ruth Marlene Fox, OSB, 1985.
of Sacred Heart Monastery in Richardton, ND.

May God bless you with a restless discomfort
about easy answers, half-truths
and superficial relationships
so that you may seek truth boldly
and love deep within your heart

May God bless you with holy anger
at injustice, oppression, and exploitation of people,
so that you may tirelessly work for
justice, freedom, and peace among all people

May God bless you with tears to shed for those
who suffer from pain, rejection, starvation and war,
so that you will reach out your hand to comfort them
and to change their pain to joy.

May God bless you with enough foolishness to believe
that you really can make a difference in this world,
so that you are able, with God's grace,
to do what others claim cannot be done.

And the blessing of God our Creator ...
these blessings are yours
– not for the asking, but for the giving
– from One who wants to be your companion, our God
... Amen

Sister Ruth Marlene Fox – Franciscan Blessing
Fox, R.M. (2016) A Franciscan Blessing. *The Almond Tree* website. https://www.thesacredbraid.com/2016/07/22/a-non-traditional-blessing/

Acknowledgments
A note of thanks to Rev Cheryl Osment, General Manager, Eastern College Australia, for allowing me to take seven weeks study leave over the summer break (2021-2), to begin this handbook, and for her constant encouragement. Thanks to Dr Art Wouters for trusting me to teach counselling, and Dr Katherine Thompson and Elise Bryant, for encouraging me to make this a practical handbook. Plus, to Kate Ryan of Writers Victoria for her editing, Dr Lyn O'Grady and Dr David Morgan for suggesting adding more worksheet prompts for counsellors. Huge thanks also to Candy Daniels and Chad Loftis for taking over my teaching, so I could finish this handbook.

Thanks to my counselling students, especially Laura Boys for her insightful conversations, her introduction and poems, and my Master of Community Counselling students, for their encouragement and inspiration along the journey. Plus, thanks to my counselling supervisor, narrative therapist Liz Morrigan, for her support over many years. Thanks also, to my dear friend Alice Jefferies for her artwork and her caring listening ear.

Special thanks to my husband Robert for his faithful support over our 50 years of marriage, and to my two sons, and grand-daughter. Plus, my mother, Shirley, in her 90s, for her help and encouragement with poetry writing.

Julie Morsillo, 2024
drjulie.morsillo@gmail.com

REFERENCES

Baird, J. (2020). Phosphorescence: On awe, wonder and things that sustain you when the world goes dark. Fourth Estate

Benstead, U. (2011) 'The shark cage': The use of metaphor with women who have experienced abuse. Psychotherapy in Australia, 17 (2), February 2011, 70-76.

Brunswick Women's Choir (2007) Seeking harmony: Stories from the Brunswick Women's Choir. See BWC website.

Chaudhury, P. & Banerjee, D. (2020). "Recovering With Nature": A Review of Ecotherapy and Implications for the COVID-19 Pandemic. Frontiers in Public Health, 10 Dec, 2020.

Chochinov, H.M. (2012) Dignity therapy: Final words for final days. Oxford University Press.

Cholbi, M. (2022). Grief: A philosophical guide. Princeton University Press.

Cooperrider, D. L., Whitney, D., & Stavros, J. M. (2003). Appreciative inquiry handbook: The first in a series of AI workbooks for leaders of change. Lakeshore Communications.

Darmody, C. (2019) Narrative walks. International Narrative Therapy and Community Work, No 1, 2019, p. 52-60.

Denborough, D. (2010). Kite of life: From intergenerational conflict to intergenerational alliance. Dulwich Centre Foundation.

Denborough, D. (2014). Retelling the stories of our lives: Everyday narrative therapy to draw inspiration and transform experience. WWNorton.

Denborough, D. Ed (2006). Trauma: Narrative responses to traumatic experiences. The Dulwich Centre, Adelaide.

Dulwich Centre. (2019) Tree of Life Projects. See website: https://dulwichcentre.com.au/the-tree-of-life/

Frankl, V. E. (1946). Man's search for meaning: An introduction to logotherapy. Beacon Press.

Fareez, M. (2015). The 'Life Certificate': A tool for grief work in Singapore. The International Journal of Narrative Therapy and Community Work. Vol 2.

Gable, S.L. & Haidt, J. (2005) What (and why) is positive psychology? Review of General Psychology, 9,2, 103-110.

Gable, S. L., & Reis, H. T. (2010). Good news! Capitalizing on positive events in an interpersonal context. In Advances in experimental social psychology (Vol. 42, pp. 195-257). Academic Press.

Gilbert, P. (2018). Introducing compassion-focused therapy. Cambridge Core. Cambridge University Press, 2 January 2018.

Ginwright, S. (2018). The future of healing: Shifting from trauma informed care to healing centered engagement. – online.

Habel, N. (1977). 'Only the jacket is my friend': On friends and redeemers in Job. Interpretation: A Journal of Bible & Theology, 31, 3.

Hegarty, T., Smith, G., & Hammersley, M (2010). Crossing the river: A metaphor for separation, liminality and reincorporation, International Journal of Narrative and Community Work, No 2.

Johnson, L. & Boyle, M. (2018). The power threat meaning framework: Overview. British Psychological Society.

Kessler, D. (2019). Finding meaning: The sixth stage of grief. Ebury Pub.

Kübler-Ross, E., & Kessler, D. (2012). On grief and grieving: Finding the meaning of grief through the five stages of loss. Scribner.

Lichter I, Mooney J, Boyd M. (1993). Biography as therapy. Palliative Medicine Research, 7(2):133-7.

Ludema, J., Cooperrider, D., & Barrett, F. (2001). Appreciative inquiry: The power of the unconditional positive question. In P. Reason & H. Bradbury (Eds.), Handbook of action research (pp. 189-199). Sage.

McAdams, D. P. (2006). The redemptive self: Stories Americans live by. Oxford University Press.

McAdams, D. (2013). The psychological self, as actor, agent and author. Perspectives on Psychological Science, May 2013. 8(3):272-295.

McMillan, D. W. (1996). Sense of community. Journal of Community Psychology, 24, 4, 315-325.

Mackay, H. (2021). The kindness revolution: How we can restore hope, rebuild trust and inspire optimism. Allen & Unwin.

Mandela, N. (2009). Long walk to freedom. Roaring Brook Press.

Maslow, A.H. (1943). Theory of Human Motivation. Psychological Review, Vol 50, p. 370-396.

Morawetz, D. (1994). Sleep better without drugs: A self-help program using Cognitive Behavioural Therapy-CBT. BookBaby.

Morsillo, J & Fisher, A. (2009). "Appreciative inquiry with migrant youth for meaningful community projects." Book chapter in M. F. Hindsworth and T. B. Lang (Eds). Community Participation and Empowerment. Nova Publishers.

Morsillo, J & Fisher, A. (2007). Appreciative inquiry with youth to create meaningful community projects. The Australian Community Psychologist, 19, pp.47;61.

Morsillo, J., & Prilleltensky, I. (2007). Social action with youth: Interventions, evaluation and psycho-political validity. Journal of Community Psychology, 35, pp.725;740.

Morsillo, J. (2004). Social action drama with same-sex attracted youth. The Community Psychologist, Summer 2004, 11;12

Neff, K. D. & Germer, C. K (2018). The mindful self-compassion workbook: A program proven way to accept yourself, find your inner strength and thrive. Guilford Press.

Nelson, G. B., & Prilleltensky, I. (2005). Community psychology: In pursuit of liberation and well-being. Palgrave Macmillan.

Oliveira, V. (2009). Team Garra: using the Team of Life to facilitate conversations with Brazilians living in Sydney. International Journal of Narrative Therapy and Community Work, (4), pp. 52–61

Prilleltensky, I. (2014). Meaning-making, mattering, and thriving in community psychology: From co-optation to amelioration and transformation. Psychosocial Intervention, 23, 2, 151-154.

Prilleltensky, I., & Prilleltensky, O. (2007). Promoting well-being: Linking personal, organizational, and community change. John Whiley & sons.

Rappaport, J. (2000). Community narratives: Tales of terror and joy. American Journal of Community Psychology, 28, p.1-24.

Rappaport, J. (1995) Empowerment meets narrative: Listening to stories and creating settings. American Journal of Community Psychology; Oct 1995; 23, 5

Rose, D.B. (1996). Nourishing Terrains: Australian Aboriginal view of landscape and wilderness. Australian Heritage Com.

Seligman M. E. P. (1991). Learned optimism: How to change your mind and your life. A.A. Knopf.

Seligman, M. (2018). PERMA™ and the building blocks of well-being. The Journal of Positive Psychology. 13 (4).

Smith, E.E. (2017). The power of meaning: Finding fulfilment in a world obsessed with happiness. Penguin.

Stockton, E. (1995). The Aboriginal Gift: Spirituality for a nation. Millennium Books, p.82.

Thompson, K. (2020). Christ-centred mindfulness: Connection to self and God. Acorn Press.

Trible, P. (1984). Texts of terror: Literary-feminist readings of Biblical narratives. Fortress Press.

Van Sambeek, L. (2024) What is 'Narrative Walks' at Metaphorically Speaking website.

Wagamese, R. (2011). One story, one song. Douglas & McIntyre.

White, M., & Epston, D. (1990). Narrative means to therapeutic ends. W. W. Norton.

White, M. (1995). Re-authoring lives: Interviews & essays. Dulwich Centre Publications.

White, M. (2007). Maps of narrative practice. W.W. Norton.

Yuen, A. (2019). Pathways beyond despair: Re-authoring lives of young people through narrative therapy. Dulwich Centre Pub.

Yuen, A. (2009). Less pain, more gain: Explorations of responses verses effects of trauma. Explorations: An E-Journal of Narrative Practice, 2, 6-16.

Useful Websites

1. Personal
Australian Counselling Association (ACA) – www.theaca.net.au
Australian Psychological Society (APS) – psychology.org.au
Beyond Blue – Dealing with depression and anxiety
 – beyondblue.org.au
Blackdog – dealing with depression
 – www.blackdoginstitute.org.au
Blue Knot Foundation – dealing with trauma - blueknot.org.au
Child counselling & support – Drummond Street Services –
 https://ds.org.au/our-services/child-counselling-support/
Compassion Focused Therapy – Dr Paul Gilbert – Compassionate
 Mind Foundation, UK – www.compassionatemind.co.uk
Dulwich Centre – Narrative Therapy origins –
 dulwichcentre.com.au
Headspace – youth mental health – headspace.org.au/
Lifeline – dealing with self-harm – www.lifeline.org.au
Metaphorically Speaking – narrative therapy & nature therapy by
 Lucy Van Sambeek – www.metaphoricallyspeaking.com.au
Mindfulness for youth – Headspace - https://headspace.org.au
Narrative Therapy – Dulwich Centre, Adelaide
 dulwichcentre.com.au
Psychotherapy & Counselling Federation Australia (PACFA)
 – https://www.pacfa.org.au
Psychological First Aid - APS & Australian Red Cross –
 psychology.org.au/getmedia/c1846704-2fa3-41ae-bf53-
 7a7451af6246/red-cross-psychological-first-aid-disasters.pdf
Reachout.com - youth wellbeing – au.reachout.com
Self-compassion – Dr Kristen Neff – mindful self-compassion
 - self-compassion.org
Rhythms of play – for meaningful fun with children -
 https://rhythmsofplay.com/
Self-compassion Program – https://self-compassion.org/the-
 program/
Soul Shepherding – spiritual care for pastors and counsellors
 – www.soulshepherding.org
St Luke's Innovative Resources, Bendigo & online
 – https://innovativeresources.org
Youth counselling – Headspace – headspace.org.au

2. Relationships
Appreciative Inquiry – Dr David Cooperrider
 – www.davidcooperrider.com/ai-process/
Autism Spectrum Australia – Aspect
 – https://www.aspect.org.au/about-autism/what-is-autism
Bounce Back Program - kids anxiety
 – www.bounceback-program.com
Bouverie Centre – healthy relationships & training
 – www.latrobe.edu.au/research/centres/health/bouverie/about
Circle of Security – parenting –
 www.circleofsecurityinternational.com
Family therapy – Bouverie Street practice & research
 – www.latrobe.edu.au/research/centres/health/bouverie
Gottman Institute - relationship issues - www.gottman.com
Open Dialogue in Australia – community approach to mental
 health – opendialogue.org.au
Reachout.com – support for youth – https://au.reachout.com
Relationships Australia - health relationships
 – relationships.org.au
Safe steps for family violence – https://www.safesteps.org.au
The Shark Cage - Ursula Benstead – protecting from abuse
 – www.ursulabenstead.com.au
 Thomas-Kilmann Conflict mode – kilmanndiagnostics.com/
1800 Respect for family violence – www.1800respect.org.au/

3. Community
Asylum Seeker Resource Centre – https://asrc.org.au
Big hART - Art & social change – www.bighart.org
Charter for Compassion – promoting world peace
 – harterforcompassion.org
Community choirs – Community Music Victoria
 – cmvic.org.au/about-us
Community Gardens Australia -
 https://communitygarden.org.au
Kindness Pandemic – www.thekindnesspandemic.org
Love makes a way – https://actionnetwork.org/groups/love-
 makes-a-way-australia
Men's Shed support programs Australia
 – mensshed.org
Neighbourhood Houses Victoria - www.nhvic.org.au
Reconciliation Australia – Australian Indigenous
 – www.reconciliation.org.au
Resilience project – GEM – Gratitude, Empathy & Mindfulness
 –//theresilienceproject.com.au/media-posts/resilience-and-
 happiness-depend-on-gratitude-empathy-and-mindfulness/
Stars Foundation – mentoring Indigenous girls to complete
 school – starsfoundation.org.au
Supports groups:
- Ask Izzy – practical help nearby - askizzy.org.au/
- Alcoholics Anonymous Australia - aa.org.au
- Narcotics Anonymous Australia - www.na.org.au/multi/
- Self-help Addiction Resource Centre - www.sharc.org.au
- Community forums for support - saneforums.org
- Suicide Line Victoria - suicideline.org.au
- Grief Australia support groups – www.grief.org.au/ga/ga/Support/Support_Groups.aspx

Tear Fund – charity addressing poverty –
 www.tearfund.org.au
Victorian Foundation for Survivors of Torture – asylum
 seekers counselling – foundationhouse.org.au

4. Nature
Australian Conservation Foundation - https://www.acf.org.au
Australian UNESCO conservation sites
 – whc.unesco.org/en/statesparties/au
CERES - Indigenous plants & nursery
 – ceres.org.au/social-enterprises/nursery-
 archive/bushfoods/
Eco-villages Australia - www.ecovillages.com.au
Forest Bathing – Shinrin Yoku Australia
 – www.shinrinyokuaustralia.com.au
Greenpeace - www.greenpeace.org.au
Sea Shepherd - www.seashepherd.org.au
Transition Australia - local sustainable communities
 – transitionaustralia.net
Trust for Nature - preserving nature with covenant property
 – trustfornature.org.au
Nature heals – alumni.berkeley.edu/california
 -magazine/online/dont-get-down-get-outside-how-awe-
 inspiring-nature-heals/
Nature-based Therapies Australia
 – naturebasedtherapies.com.au
Narrative Walks – Metaphorically speaking
 – www.metaphoricallyspeaking.com.au/narrative-
 walks/#:~:text=During%20the%20walk%20participants%
 20reflect,work%20on%20during%20the%20walk.

Video Links

Page 7 – Richard Wagamese – Matt Cohen Award speech 2015- https://youtube/t0z9rYHbQ8E?si=G-Ir14CZM_Y1NCbZ

Page 8 – President Nelson Mandela - inaugural speech (1994) -https://www.youtube.com/watch?v=pJiXu4q__VU

Page 8 – Dan McAdams lecture - *Narrative approaches to the self (2022)* - www.youtube.com/watch?v=C1eEpK23Hvg

Page 8 – Viktor Frankl interview - *Why meaning matters (1963)* - www.youtube.com/watch?v=BB8X-Go7lgw

Page 9 – Julie Morsillo presentation trailer - Counselling after disasters seminar (2020) - www.youtube.com/watch?v=kBuH29ScVjg

Page 11 – Julie Morsillo interview - What is community psychology? (2014) - www.youtube.com/watch?v=kBuH29ScVjg

Page 15 – David Treleaven Anchors video– *Trauma-Sensitive Mindfulness by (2021)* – www.youtube.com/watch?v=C4YUs2OC-LQ

Page 18 – Stephanie Smilas – Morning stretches (2019) - www.youtube.com/watch?v=u737fA2JWnY

Page 20 – Martin Seligman – *The new era on positive psychology Ted Talk (2008)* – www.ted.com/talks/martin_seligman_the_new_era_of_positive_psychology?trigger=5s

Page 21 – Music Therapy in Australia & New Zealand video (2013) – www.youtube.com/watch?v=4pCEBKxec8w

Page 21 – Nordoff-Robbins Music Therapy Australia (2018) – www.youtube.com/watch?v=3i41HswYLQU

Page 21 – Angel Yuen talk– Co-discovering hope with children facing hardships (2021) - www.youtube.com/watch?v=eo7RwdfVtV4

Page 22 – Isaac Prilleltensky Ted Talk – *Community Wellbeing: Socialize or social lies (2010)* - www.youtube.com/watch?v=WJlx8CI-rRg

Page 22 – Isaac Prilleltensky– *Mattering, Happiness, and Wellbeing (2024)* – www.youtube.com/watch?v=iluUHZnjMsw

Page 23 – Abraham Maslow lecture - Further reaches of human nature (1967) – www.youtube.com/watch?v=pagvjnTEEvg

Page 23 – Julian Rappaport: Empowerment concepts (2018) - www.youtube.com/watch?v=yrimm5JScQY

Page 24 – Shawn Ginwright – Healing centred engagement www.youtube.com/watch?v=GKItZaF6Wb0

Page 25 – Loretta Pederson – Narrative Therapy: Acts of resistance & acts of reclaiming (2018) – www.youtube.com/watch?v=ftCAmkYnAY4

Page 26 – Emily E Smith – *The power of meaning: Crafting a life that matters (2018)* – www.youtube.com/watch?v=9bVl4xdPUns

Page 27 – Emily E Smith - *How to build four pillars of meaning for flourishing life (2022)* - www.youtube.com/watch?v=9bVl4xdPUns

Page 27 – *Let's talk about mental health podcast (2024)* www.youtube.com/watch?v=3QPw57KlF1U

Page 29 – Caron Baginski: How to start a gratitude journal - www.youtube.com/watch?v=GZghu_xFRM8

Page 32 – David Kessler - *How to heal from grief by changing your story (2023)* - www.youtube.com/watch?v=YroTNH1lIvo

Page 33 – David Kessler Ted Talk - *How to find meaning after loss (2021)* – www.youtube.com/watch?v=D3azoUEEy3E

Page 34 – Dan McAdams – *Narrative approaches to the self* -www.youtube.com/watch?v=C1eEpK23Hvg

Page 34 – Dan McAdams – *Narrative Identity & the constructed imagination* - www.youtube.com/watch?v=h5noiP9VD4U

Page 37 – David Denborough – *Exchanging stories, skills and songs* - www.youtube.com/watch?v=hU1-DL8jRHY

Page 38 – Sunny Millar Ted Talk – *Life with gender dysphoria (2018)* - www.youtube.com/watch?v=M9YICZZeJNs

Page 38 – Royal Children's Hospital – *Gender Service: trans & gender diverse* - www.rch.org.au/adolescent-medicine/gender-service/

Page 40 – Michael White – *Trauma & Narrative Therapy (2007)* -https://vimeo.com/34671797

Page 40 – David Epston – *How do we come to know whose who seek our help? (2021)* - www.youtube.com/watch?v=oNUxWBRjb7A

Page 41 – Anees Hakim – Using the Tree of Life tool to talk about stories of hope and resilience (2020 – www.youtube.com/watch?v=rkPcXu_4sds

Page 42 – *Tree of Life: Working with vulnerable children (2022)* – www.youtube.com/watch?v=L9gVKMxjUvU

Page 43 – David Denborough: Tree of Life (2024) -www.youtube.com/watch?v=K5u5SdsNdkY

Page 44 – *Team of Life - Offering young people a sporting chance (2024)* - www.youtube.com/watch?v=K5u5SdsNdkY

Page 45 – *Kite of Life: Intergenerational conflict to alliance (2011)* - https://vimeo.com/18946312

Page 49 – *Narrative therapy - Life Certificate for grief & loss (2018)* – www.youtube.com/watch?v=HImiFzdRfCY

Page 51 – Christopher Germer- *Mindful self-compassion (2020)* - www.youtube.com/watch?v=igOBO1RfUtc

Page 52 – Kristin Neff – *Mindfulness & Self-compassion (2013)* - www.youtube.com/watch?v=qqQHhF4CaKQ

Page 53: Paul Gilbert – *How mindfulness fosters compassion (2013)* – www.youtube.com/watch?v=pz9Fr_v9Okw

Page 54 – Paul Gilbert - *Compassion Focused Therapy workshop (2013)*- www.youtube.com/watch?v=qnHuECDlSvE

Page 55 – Julie Morsillo - *Faith and Identity (2018)* -https://ultimateyouthworkcr.com.au/2018/05/faith-and-identity/?_ga=2.255432960.901461188.1720142354-2054609077.1720142354

Page 56 – Kristin Neff Ted Talk – *Self-esteem & self-compassion (2013)* www.youtube.com/watch?v=IvtZBUSplr4

Page 57 – Catherine Barrett – The Kindness Pandemic (2020) - www.youtube.com/watch?v=WVPaQ_0P9XM

Page 59 – Hugh Mackay – The joy of discovering who we really are (2020) – www.youtube.com/watch?v=nntiR-H-PC0

Page 63 – Jane Bavineau – *A skeptic's guide to Appreciative inquiry* (2018) - www.youtube.com/watch?v=UfUm-6K1DRA

Page 66 – Ursula Benstead – *The Shark Cage metaphor & framework (2021)* – www.youtube.com/watch?v=QW7kqvY4ruw

Page 67 – *ABC News* - What is coercive control in domestic violence relationships? *(2021)* – www.youtube.com/watch?v=lMPh6dcvMtY

Page 69 - Power Threat Meaning Framework webinar by Dr Lucy Johnstone – www.youtube.com/watch?v=WXrHGxVJSng

Page 70 – *Lucy Johnstone* – Power Threat Meaning Framework *(2023)* - www.youtube.com/watch?v=WXrHGxVJSng

Page 71 – John Gottman – The science of love Ted Talk (2018) – www.youtube.com/watch?v=-uazFBCDvVw

Page 71– *Social Skills Coaching* - Active & Constructive Responding *(2024)* – www.youtube.com/watch?v=X1UxnMv2BRg

Page 73 – Lewis Psychology – Compassion Focused Therapy (2020) – www.youtube.com/watch?v=yr6TZE6XTg4

Page 75– Harvey Chochinov – *Dignity at the end of life (2023)* – www.youtube.com/watch?v=hA0YP4QJJd4

Page 78 – *Erika Sanbourne* – What is sense of community? *(2021)* – www.youtube.com/watch?v=Moa943MVQWg

Page 78 – *Port Adelaide* – Neighbourhood Day: Creating a sense of community *(2022)* – www.youtube.com/watch?v=qvOSplLWx9Q

Page 79 – *Bankwest Curtin* – Stronger together: Loneliness and social connectedness *(2021)* – www.youtube.com/watch?v=aN3u24Bxwk4

Page 80 – Community Refugee Sponsorship Aust – Community-led support for refugees in Australia (2021) – www.youtube.com/watch?v=nvpAHpAczdA

Page 80 – ABC Australia Backroads – Improve mental health with art & fitness (2022) – www.youtube.com/watch?v=hhqmgIRLRmM

Page 82 – Brunswick Women's Choir video (2018) – www.youtube.com/watch?v=ZyTW5J9sDOs

Page 83 - *Gardening Australia* - Growing veggies and friendships *(2021)* - www.youtube.com/watch?v=DtsGaaTbJ6o

Page 83 – *Gardening Australia* – Unused public space to community farm *(2022)* – www.youtube.com/watch?v=yT0FPs6dPvE

Page 83 – *ABC Australia video* – Craft group donates handmade good to vulnerable communities *(2020)* – www.youtube.com/watch?v=AYG-vA1xHB8

Page 83 – *Relationships Australia* – Building community resilience after natural disasters *(2023)* – www.youtube.com/watch?v=WFI_Q7-IKxw

Page 84 – *ABC News* – *Helping newcomers forge strong connections, (2021)* – www.youtube.com/watch?v=F60q1Q7LQcQ

Page 86 – Deborah Bird Rose – *Country and the gift* (Sydney Environment Institute, 2014) – www.youtube.com/watch?v=suSbvoAw0g4

Page 86 – ABC TV – Back to Nature (2021) – www.youtube.com/watch?v=DAGBVE3V4s0

Page 87 - Gardening Australia - Garden project for inclusive community connection (2024) – www.youtube.com/watch?v=fylPhREMymo

Page 87 – Permaculture Magazine – Eco-village Pioneers (2010) – www.youtube.com/watch?v=1m5rSTVIV-A

Page 88 – Back to Nature ABC TV – Health benefits of nature video (2021) – www.youtube.com/watch?v=19T26Qunxf8

Page 89 – Life of Kotts – The Japanese art of Forest Bathing (2021) – www.youtube.com/watch?v=5L8mEU40Gjs

Page 90 – Bronwyn Paynter – Forest Bathing in Deep Creek National Park (2020) – www.youtube.com/watch?v=U344VH0pAl0

Page 93 - Zart Australia Art - Coral Reef Collage (2023) www.youtube.com/watch?v=khpkEiqtnDM

Page 93 – Artist-Gardener, ABC Australia Podcast (2020) – www.youtube.com/watch?v=fpf5EeQu75U

Poems & Permissions

Poems by Dr Julie Morsillo

1. Finding redemption after loss (2022) – page 9
2. Juliette finds courage (2015) – page 10
3. Walk in the park (2024) – page 14
4. Grandpa's bush hideaway (2015) – page 28
5. Granny Jane is stolen (2016) – page 31
6. Can Grumpy Gum survive? (2012) – page 35
7. Song of hope (2010) – page 36
8. Tough tattooed girl (2021) – page 37
9. Distraught father (2021) – page 38
10. My prayer song (1983) – page 55
11. Pandemic to rock the world (2021) – page 57
12. Fly away song (1999) – page 72
13. Peace song (1984) – page 77
14. Song of community (2020) – page 79

Poems & prose by Laura Boys

1. Finding redemptive stories (2021) – page 6
2. Stories have power (2021) – page 7
3. You are perfect in every way (2021) – page 56
4. Gift of friendship (2021) – page 73

Copyright acknowledgements

Narrative therapy metaphors, copyright@2024 by Dulwich Centre Publications, https://dulwichcentre.com.au, used with permission. Narrative therapy Tree of Life drawing, copyright@2024 by Juliet Young, Creative Clinical Psychologist, www.julietyoung.co.uk/, used with permission. Positive psychology PERMA™ trademark used with permission from Dr Martin Seligman. Power of Meaning four pillars concept, copyright@2017 by Dr Emily E Smith, used with permission. The Psychological Self table, copyright@2013 by Dr Dan McAdams, reprinted with permission. Self-compassion exercises, copyright @2024 by Dr Kristin Neff, https://self-compassion.org/, used with permission. The Shark Cage concept, copyright@2017 by Ursula Benstead, www.ursulabenstead.com.au, used with permission. The Power Threat Meaning Framework concept, copyright@2017 by British Psychological Society, www.bps.org.uk/, used with permission. Conflict model diagram, Copyright © 2009–2024 by Kilmann Diagnostics LLC. All rights reserved. Original figure is available at: http://www.kilmanndiagnostics.com/overview-thomas-kilmann-conflict-mode-instrument-tki.

Every effort has been made to trace copyright holders in all the copyrighted materials in this handbook. The Publisher regrets any oversight and will be pleased to rectify any omission in future editions.#